IMPROVING THE NATION'S

WATER SECURITY

OPPORTUNITIES FOR RESEARCH

D1643247

Committee on Water System Security Research

Water Science and Technology Board

Division on Earth and Life Studies

NATIONAL RESEARCH COUNCIL
OF THE NATIONAL ACADEMIES

THE NATIONAL ACADEMIES PRESS
Washington, D.C.
www.nap.edu

THE NATIONAL ACADEMIES PRESS 500 Fifth Street, N.W. Washington, DC 20001

NOTICE: The project that is the subject of this report was approved by the Governing Board of the National Research Council, whose members are drawn from the councils of the National Academy of Sciences, the National Academy of Engineering, and the Institute of Medicine. The members of the panel responsible for the report were chosen for their special competences and with regard for appropriate balance.

Support for this study was provided by the Environmental Protection Agency under Contract Number 68-C-03-081. Any opinions, findings, conclusions, or recommendations expressed in this publication are those of the author(s) and do not necessarily reflect the views of the organizations or agencies that provided support for the project.

International Standard Book Number-13: 978-0-309-10566-8
International Standard Book Number-10: 0-309-10566-8

Additional copies of this report are available from the National Academies Press, 500 Fifth Street, N.W., Lockbox 285, Washington, DC 20055; (800) 624-6242 or (202) 334-3313 (in the Washington metropolitan area); Internet, http://www.nap.edu.

Copyright 2007 by the National Academy of Sciences. All rights reserved.

Printed in the United States of America.

THE NATIONAL ACADEMIES
Advisers to the Nation on Science, Engineering, and Medicine

The **National Academy of Sciences** is a private, nonprofit, self-perpetuating society of distinguished scholars engaged in scientific and engineering research, dedicated to the furtherance of science and technology and to their use for the general welfare. Upon the authority of the charter granted to it by the Congress in 1863, the Academy has a mandate that requires it to advise the federal government on scientific and technical matters. Dr. Ralph J. Cicerone is president of the National Academy of Sciences.

The **National Academy of Engineering** was established in 1964, under the charter of the National Academy of Sciences, as a parallel organization of outstanding engineers. It is autonomous in its administration and in the selection of its members, sharing with the National Academy of Sciences the responsibility for advising the federal government. The National Academy of Engineering also sponsors engineering programs aimed at meeting national needs, encourages education and research, and recognizes the superior achievements of engineers. Dr. Charles M. Vest is president of the National Academy of Engineering.

The **Institute of Medicine** was established in 1970 by the National Academy of Sciences to secure the services of eminent members of appropriate professions in the examination of policy matters pertaining to the health of the public. The Institute acts under the responsibility given to the National Academy of Sciences by its congressional charter to be an adviser to the federal government and, upon its own initiative, to identify issues of medical care, research, and education. Dr. Harvey V. Fineberg is president of the Institute of Medicine.

The **National Research Council** was organized by the National Academy of Sciences in 1916 to associate the broad community of science and technology with the Academy's purposes of furthering knowledge and advising the federal government. Functioning in accordance with general policies determined by the Academy, the Council has become the principal operating agency of both the National Academy of Sciences and the National Academy of Engineering in providing services to the government, the public, and the scientific and engineering communities. The Council is administered jointly by both Academies and the Institute of Medicine. Dr. Ralph J. Cicerone and Dr. Charles M. Vest are chair and vice chair, respectively, of the National Research Council.

www.national-academies.org

COMMITTEE ON WATER SYSTEM
SECURITY RESEARCH[*]

DAVID M. OZONOFF, *Chair*, Boston University School of Public Health, Boston, Massachusetts
FRANCIS A. DIGIANO, University of North Carolina, Chapel Hill
CHARLES N. HAAS, Drexel University, Philadelphia, Pennsylvania
ANNA K. HARDING, Oregon State University, Corvallis
DENNIS D. JURANEK, Centers for Disease Control and Prevention, retired, Atlanta, Georgia
NANCY K. KIM, New York State Department of Health, Albany
BRUCE M. LARSON, American Water, Vorhees, New Jersey
DANIEL V. LIM, University of South Florida, Tampa
RUDOLPH V. MATALUCCI, Rudolph Matalucci Consultants, Inc., Albuquerque, New Mexico
DAVID A. RECKHOW, University of Massachusetts, Amherst
H. GERARD SCHWARTZ, JR., Sverdup Civil, Inc., retired, St. Louis, Missouri
JOHN P. SULLIVAN, Boston Water and Sewer Commission, Massachusetts
GEORGE TCHOBANOGLOUS, University of California, Davis, Emeritus

NRC Staff

STEPHANIE E. JOHNSON, Study Director (From March 2005)
LAURA J. EHLERS, Study Director (Until March 2005)
DOROTHY K. WEIR, Research Associate

---

[*]The activities of this committee were overseen and supported by the National Research Council's Water Science and Technology Board (see Appendix B for listing). Biographical information on committee members and staff is contained in Appendix C.

Preface

The events of September 11, 2001, changed perceptions and rearranged priorities in many ways. In the wake of the 2001 attacks, the U.S. Environmental Protection Agency (EPA), as the lead agency in securing the nation's water infrastructure, developed and began to implement a research and technical support program in drinking water and wastewater security. In 2003, in response to the EPA's request, the National Research Council's (NRC's) Water Science and Technology Board convened the Panel on Water System Security Research to review the agency's draft Water Security Research and Technical Support Action Plan (Action Plan). Two reports were issued (see NRC, 2004) to help the EPA identify important issues and needs and to make recommendations for improvement.

Much has now been accomplished in the way of filling the most obvious short-term information gaps, but water security research will need to be a continuous effort because water security needs and emphases will necessarily change as conditions, knowledge, technologies, and the industry change. As a consequence, the EPA's National Homeland Security Research Center (NHSRC) has been made permanent, and in 2004, the EPA sought additional assistance from the NRC in evaluating progress to date and framing a mid- to long-range water security research strategy. The NRC organized the Committee on Water System Security Research for this purpose, and we present its final report here.[1]

The committee met five times over the span of two years. The first two meetings were held in Cincinnati, Ohio, at the headquarters of the NHSRC. At these meetings, the committee members were able to obtain information from relevant EPA water security research personnel and review classified material as necessary. We received outstanding coop-

---

[1] The committee also issued an interim letter report in November 2005 that is included in Appendix A.

eration from EPA personnel, and we would particularly like to thank Kim Fox, Jon Herrmann, and Scott Minamyer for their help in addressing the committee's information needs.

The committee's charge was broad and relatively nonspecific, which allowed considerable latitude, even though this latitude created its own organizational challenges. The task of reviewing a continually evolving research program also presented difficulties for the committee. Throughout, however, the committee was mindful of its chief objective: to help the EPA in the difficult task of fashioning a reasonable, practical, and useful agenda for research and technical support in water and wastewater security. We began with a good appreciation for the difficulty of the task and that appreciation only grew as we learned more about the research program and its inherent challenges.

The committee consisted of 13 members with scientific, technical, public policy, utilities management, and social science expertise. The committee was not only hardworking but also remarkably collegial and congenial, making a hard job easier as a result. As chair, I would like to thank committee members personally for making the job as pleasurable as it could be and producing a solid, thoughtfully developed report. No NRC report is possible, however, without expert staff, for whom words like "extraordinary" are commonplace. Commonplace or not, this committee was blessed by truly extraordinary staff. Our study director, Dr. Stephanie Johnson, kept us focused, guided our discussions, and used her considerable experience and knowledge to avoid problems and move us in the most fruitful directions. Our project assistant, Dorothy Weir, made sure logistics, research assistance, and editorial tasks were done transparently, and her keen mind helped substantively as well.

This report has been reviewed in draft form by individuals chosen for their diverse perspectives and technical expertise, in accordance with procedures approved by the NRC's Report Review Committee. The purpose of this independent review is to provide candid and critical comments that will assist the NRC in making its published report as sound as possible and will ensure that the report meets institutional standards for objectivity, evidence, and responsiveness to the study charge. The review comments and draft manuscript remain confidential to protect the integrity of the deliberative process. We wish to thank the following individuals for their review of this report: Frank Blaha, American Water Works Association Research Foundation; Frank Bove, Agency for Toxic Substances and Disease Registry; William Cooper, University of California, Irvine; William Desing, CH2M Hill; Eve Hinman, Hinman Consulting Engineers, Inc.; Kerry Kirk Pflugh, New Jersey Department of Environmental Protection; David Spath, California Department of Health Services; Mic Stewart, Metropolitan Water District of Southern California; and Walter Weber, University of Michigan.

Although the reviewers listed above have provided many constructive comments and suggestions, they were not asked to endorse the conclusions or recommendations, nor did they see the final draft of the report before its release. The review of this report was overseen by Marylynn Yates of the University of California, Riverside. Appointed by the NRC, she was responsible for making certain that an independent examination of this report was carried out in accordance with institutional procedures and that all review comments were considered carefully. Responsibility for the final content of this report rests entirely with the authoring committee and the institution.

David M. Ozonoff, *Chair*

Contents

Summary

Concern over terrorist attacks since 2001 has directed attention to potential vulnerabilities of the nation's water and wastewater systems as targets of malicious attacks. An attack on the water infrastructure could cause mortality, injury, or sickness; large-scale environmental impacts; and a loss of public confidence in the safety and quality of drinking water supplies.

Since 1998, the Environmental Protection Agency (EPA) has served as the lead agency for coordinating efforts to protect the water sector—one of the nation's critical infrastructures—from intentional attacks. In 2002, the EPA initiated a research program to address immediate research and technical support needs for water and wastewater security. Working together, the EPA's Office of Research and Development (ORD) and Office of Water developed a focused plan (the Water Security Research and Technical Support Action Plan) with a three- to four-year time frame, consistent with the originally envisioned lifespan of the ORD's National Homeland Security Research Center (NHSRC). Although the plan included some original research, most research projects were narrowly conceived and emphasized the mining of existing data, making information available in a more useful and accessible format, and evaluating tools and technologies for water system security. When it became clear there was much more required than could be addressed in the short term, the NHSRC was made permanent and the Water Infrastructure Protection Division was formed.

Near the end of the planning time frames used in the Action Plan, the EPA requested a National Research Council (NRC) study to assist in strategic planning for a permanent research program with a long-term vision. A committee was formed by the NRC's Water Science and Technology Board to review progress by the EPA on its water security activities, including the Action Plan; to identify and evaluate the importance of short- and long-term research needs; and to identify opportunities for improved coordination and communication of the results (see Chapter 1 for complete statement of task). In this report, the committee evaluates research progress to date, analyzes lessons learned from the first four years, and looks ahead to a vision of the EPA's water security research program with specific recommendations for strengthening it.

The committee developed four criteria to guide its evaluation of the value of the EPA's water security research projects and to provide a foundation for its recommendations for future research priorities:

1. Water security threats with the greatest likelihood and potential consequences (including fatalities, sickness, economic losses, and loss of public confidence) are addressed.
2. The effectiveness and efficiency of the nation's response and recovery capacity are improved and/or risk reduction or consequence mitigation measures are developed.
3. Implementation of new technologies/methodologies is judged to be likely, taking into account their cost, usefulness, and maintenance requirements.
4. Dual-use benefits accrue from the research.

For this report, "dual use" refers to research that addresses both security concerns and other important water infrastructure objectives (e.g., routine monitoring, protection from natural hazards). Dual-use benefits are included among these criteria because they significantly improve the likelihood of implementation of the research products and their benefits, but the committee does not view dual use as an absolute requirement for all water security research.

The EPA has shown leadership and initiative in the area of water security research. Although it is too early to judge the success of the water security research program, progress has been made toward addressing critical knowledge gaps. To sustain its leadership role, the EPA should develop a strategic plan with long-term research program objectives, address gaps in expertise among EPA program managers and researchers, and improve its approaches to information dissemination. Specific recommendations are also provided for short- and long-term priorities for water security research.

EVALUATION OF THE EPA'S RESEARCH PROGRESS

Many of the projects have been delayed beyond the originally anticipated timelines and, thus, relatively few products were publicly released during the time frame of the committee's review. Nevertheless, progress has been made in implementing the EPA's water security research and technical support program described in the Action Plan (see Chapter 4). The committee was tasked to evaluate progress, not the effectiveness and success of the program, which would not have been feasible at this point. Overall, the EPA water security program has initiated research and technical support projects that address some important issues and critical gaps in knowledge. With proper continued management, these projects could yield results that will be useful for improving the nation's water security and its response and recovery capacity if the findings reach those who need them in a timely way. Many of the EPA projects under way also have valuable dual-use benefits, which makes dissemination of results in a useful form all the more important.

Tools have been developed and information generated in several key areas. Priority contaminants have been identified, and this process has served as a means to prioritize the EPA's other research efforts. Numerous tools have been developed, including a contaminant information database, an exposure assessment tool, and refined distribution system models that will help users improve their terrorism preparedness and response capabilities. Protocols for contaminant analysis have been identified or developed, and research is under way to test the application of current real-time monitoring system technologies, appropriately emphasizing nonspecific detection devices with dual-use applications. Risk communication strategies have been developed and communication workshops held to improve response strategies in case of a water security event. Basic laboratory research is also under way to identify surrogates and to fill critical gaps in the current understanding of the fate and transport and exposure risks for water security agents. Among the EPA's implementation activities, modifications have been made to the Technology Testing and Evaluation Program (TTEP) that should improve both the effectiveness of the process and the value of the results to end users.

Other areas, such as physical and cyber security, contingency planning, and wastewater security, have shown weaker or somewhat disjointed progress. The EPA's lack of expertise in these areas has meant that much of the work has taken place outside the EPA, and contract management alone affords limited oversight and guidance.

An important overarching issue that remains unresolved is making water security information accessible to those who might need it. The problem of information sharing in a security context is one of the most difficult the EPA faces. Currently, some important information on priority contaminants and threats that could improve utilities' response capabilities has been classified and cannot be shared with utilities, even through secure dissemination mechanisms.

RECOMMENDATIONS FOR IMPROVING PROGRAM IMPLEMENTATION

Thoughtful research management planning is essential as the EPA moves forward to build a long-term research program in water security. To strengthen the EPA's water security research program and utilize its limited resources in the best way, several recommendations for improving program implementation are provided.

The NHSRC's Water Infrastructure Protection Division should formally articulate its mission and program objectives as it moves beyond the short-term time frame of the Action Plan. To enhance a vision for future research, the committee presents three strategic objectives for organizing future water security research initiatives, emphasizing research products that can guide pre-incident, incident, and post-incident water security activities. Within these objectives, priority setting will be necessary, and several criteria are presented in Chapter 5. A strategic planning exercise is a logical and necessary extension of the Action Plan that will strengthen the EPA's leadership in the field. The EPA will need to investigate existing planning and decision-making models before embarking on this endeavor to ensure a successful and appropriately inclusive planning process.

The EPA should develop greater in-house research capability, or at least subject matter expertise, in disciplines that have been historically weak at the EPA but where long-term water security concerns are projected. Now that the NHSRC has been made permanent, it should reassess the pros and cons of using contracts as the principal management tool for conducting research in many of the areas the EPA is not currently staffed or equipped to handle. Based on the advantages of extramural funding, the EPA should continue to use contract mechansims to support some water security research, but careful attention should be given to achieving the right balance with in-house expertise. When research is conducted via contracts, the EPA still needs adequate in-house expertise to evaluate and manage such contracts.

The NHSRC should explore alternatives to improve independent peer review of sensitive or classified work. A major challenge is independent peer review of water security research products that contain classified, or sensitive but unclassified, material. Effective independent peer review is an important mechanism for avoiding research errors, program problems, and inefficiencies, but sensitive and classified materials and products make peer review difficult, and currently, peer review mechanisms within the NHSRC may not be sufficient. Therefore, the EPA should carefully review areas where independent peer review involving sensitive and classified material is needed and examine available mechanisms for accomplishing peer review, such as those used by other federal agencies.

The NHSRC should solicit early input and involvement from its priority audiences to improve the effectiveness of its research communication. Communication strategies are more likely to be effective if target audiences are asked for input *prior* to the communication effort. This can be accomplished by characterizing specific audiences in advance, getting input from audiences prior to developing a communication effort, pretesting materials on an intended audience, and soliciting feedback on communication efforts during early phases of implementation. These efforts save resources by ensuring research products are effective and reach those who need them. If the products of research are not used, the resources expended to produce them are ultimately wasted.

The NHSRC should improve its approaches to information dissemination, using both security-specific communication mechanisms and broadly applicable portal technology. The EPA wishes to make its research products widely available to the water sector, and the committee encourages this practice. However, current Web-based approaches to dissemination need to be improved because the number of anticipated research products will undoubtedly make it difficult for utilities to keep up with the information. Use of security-specific mechanisms (e.g., the Water Information Sharing and Analysis Center [WaterISAC], Water Security Channel, Homeland Security Information Network) would enable the EPA to reach out to a large portion of its intended audience and facilitate direct notification about recently published material. The EPA should continue to use the WaterISAC to alert stakeholders to the availability of sensitive materials. The EPA should also consider developing a Web-based information portal to make the research findings easily and readily accessible to the full range of stakeholders. Feedback mechanisms should be developed to learn what products have been especially useful and what improvements may be needed.

The EPA should consider methods to disseminate important but sensitive security information. The EPA should analyze the costs and benefits of keeping information secure and, if necessary, find ways to communicate important information from sensitive or classified research products so that the research can be useful to stakeholders who need it. The EPA should also consider options for releasing classified or "for official use only" information that could improve response and recovery at the time of a water security emergency.

The EPA water security research will only reduce risk if the products are made available to and properly utilized by utilities; local, state, and federal response agencies; and the public. Therefore, the above recommendations on improving communication and addressing information security barriers are critical to the success of the research program and should be the agency's highest priorities.

RECOMMENDATIONS FOR FUTURE RESEARCH DIRECTIONS

Based on the committee's review of the EPA's water security research progress in Chapter 4 and the criteria developed in Chapter 3, two key water security research gaps—behavioral science and innovative water and wastewater infrastructure designs—are identified that were not considered in the short-term planning horizon of the Action Plan. To address these gaps, **the EPA should develop a program of interdisciplinary empirical research in behavioral science to better understand how to prepare stakeholders for water security incidents.** The EPA should take advantage of existing behavioral science research that could be applied to water security issues to improve response and recovery efforts. At the same time, when gaps exist, the EPA should support rigorous empirical research that will help address, for example, what the public's beliefs, opinions, and knowledge about water security risks are; how risk perception and other psychological factors affect responses to water-related events; and how to communicate these risks effectively to the public. **The EPA should also take a leadership role in providing guidance for the planning, design, and implementation of new, more sustainable and resilient water and wastewater facilities for the 21st century.** Given the investments necessary to upgrade and sustain the country's water and wastewater systems, research on innovative approaches to make the infrastructure more sustainable and resilient both to routine and malicious incidents would provide substantial dual-use benefits. The EPA should help develop and test new concepts, technologies, and management structures for water and wastewater utilities to meet objectives of public health, sustainability, cost-effectiveness, and homeland security.

Specific short- and long-term water security research recommendations are presented in Chapter 6 in three areas: (1) developing products to support more resilient design and operation of facilities and systems, (2) improving the ability of operators and responders to detect and assess incidents, and (3) improving response and recovery. Recommended research topics in the area of supporting more resilient design and operation of systems include improved methods for risk assessment and innovative designs for water and wastewater systems. **Physical and cyber threats specifically deserve more attention and analysis because this information could influence EPA's future research priorities and utilities' preparedness and response planning.**

Research suggestions that improve the ability of operators and responders to detect and assess incidents build upon the EPA's current research in the areas of analytical methodologies, monitoring, and distribution system modeling. To support the simulation models in development, a substantial amount of fundamental research is needed to improve understanding of the fate and transport of contaminants in distribution systems. Based on the number of emerging technologies and agents of interest, the EPA should develop a prioritization strategy for technology testing to optimize the resources devoted to this effort.

Recommendations for future research priorities to improve response and recovery emphasize the sustainability of tools for emergency planning and response and improving research on water security contingencies, behavioral sciences, and risk communication. The EPA should also evaluate the relative importance of future laboratory work on surrogate development and address data gaps in the knowledge of decontamination processes and behavior. So far, the EPA has not taken advantage of the many opportunities from Hurricane Katrina to harvest lessons learned related to response and recovery, despite encouragement provided by this committee in NRC (2005; see Appendix A), and the window of opportunity is rapidly closing.

Some of the committee's research recommendations lie outside of the EPA's traditional areas of expertise. The EPA will, therefore, need to consider how best to balance intramural and extramural approaches to carry out the research, while maintaining appropriate oversight and input into research activities. Increasing staff expertise in some key areas, such as physical security and behavioral sciences, will be necessary to build a strong and well-rounded water security research program.

1

Introduction

The concern over terrorist attacks of recent years has raised awareness of the vulnerability of the nation's critical infrastructures, including water systems, and has accelerated activities to improve water security. In September 2002, the Environmental Protection Agency (EPA) formed the National Homeland Security Research Center[1] (NHSRC) to manage, coordinate, and support research and technical assistance in the area of homeland security, with a major initiative related to protection of the nation's water and wastewater infrastructure.

This report provides a review of the progress of the NHSRC's water security[2] research and technical support activities and makes recommendations for strengthening the research program. In this introductory chapter, the scope of security threats to water and wastewater systems, the role of science and technology in countering terrorism, and the EPA's role in drinking water and wastewater security research are discussed. The chapter concludes with the committee's charge to set the context for this report.

SCOPE OF SECURITY THREATS TO WATER AND WASTEWATER SYSTEMS

Safety and reliability have always been important to water and wastewater utilities, but the scope and scale of threats from terrorism have increased attention to issues of security. While contingency plans have existed for decades within the water and wastewater utilities industry to handle power interruptions or natural events such as flooding, new security concerns include disruption of service by physical attack (e.g.,

---

[1] For further information on the NHSRC, please see *http://www.epa.gov/nhsrc/about.htm*.
[2] In this report, the term "water security" is considered to include drinking water and wastewater security issues.

explosives), breaches in cyber security, and the intentional release of contaminants (including chemical, biological, and radiological agents).

Both drinking water and wastewater systems are vulnerable to terrorist attack. The consequences of security threats involve potential mortality, injury, or sickness; economic losses; extended periods of service interruption; and a loss of public confidence in the safety and quality of drinking water supplies—a major concern even without a serious public health consequence. Flushing a drinking water distribution system in response to intentional chemical contamination could transport contaminants to the wastewater system and, unless removed by wastewater treatment, into receiving waters; thus, large-scale environmental impacts could also result from water security events.

Security threats to wastewater systems, while posing a less direct impact on public health, are nevertheless serious concerns. Chemical or microbial agents added in relatively small quantities to a wastewater system could disrupt the treatment process, and a physical attack on a wastewater collection system could create local public health concerns and potentially large-scale environmental impacts. Wastewater collection systems (e.g., large-diameter sewer mains) may also serve as conduits for malicious attacks via explosives that could cause a large number of injuries and fatalities. An attack on a wastewater system could also create public health concerns if untreated wastewater were discharged to a river used as a downstream drinking water supply or for recreational purposes (e.g., swimming, fishing).

Threats to water security also raise concerns regarding cross-sector interdependencies of critical infrastructures. Water utilities are largely dependent upon electric power to treat and distribute water. Likewise, electric power is essential to collect and treat wastewater, although diesel power generators can be used in the short term. The firefighting ability of municipalities would be seriously weakened without an adequate and uninterrupted supply of water, and intentional fires could be set as part of a terrorist attack to further exacerbate this impact. Explosive attacks in wastewater collection systems could affect other critical colocated infrastructures, such as communications.

Many of the principles used to prepare for and to respond to water security threats are directly applicable to natural hazards. Hurricane Katrina reminded the nation that natural disasters can cause both physical damage and contamination impacts on water and wastewater systems. Moreover, natural disasters (e.g., earthquakes, floods) and routine system problems (e.g., aging infrastructure, nonintentional contamination events) are far more likely to occur than a terrorist attack. An epidemic or pandemic illness could also create failures in smaller water or waste-water utilities if supply chains become compromised due to widespread absenteeism or if essential personnel are incapacitated. Thus, threats from intentional attacks are not the only threats to the integrity of the nation's water systems. However, preparing for and securing systems against intentional threats also mitigates the impacts of some nonintentional threats and heightens awareness of vulnerabilities of all kinds.

ROLE OF SCIENCE AND TECHNOLOGY IN COUNTERING TERRORISM

The threat of terrorism has prompted research and development of technologies to detect attacks on water systems as well as to decontaminate and restore water systems after an attack. Technological advances have much to offer in new sensing, surveillance, and protection strategies, but these technologies cannot prevent an attack from occurring. The principal efforts aimed at countering terrorism will, as always, rely on diplomacy, international relations, intelligence gathering, and international policy. Technological advances can help prevent or mitigate further harm should an attack take place, although they may also bring unacceptable or unsustainable costs. A National Research Council (NRC) committee concluded in *Making the Nation Safer* (NRC, 2002) that "the role of technology can be overstated." A well-reasoned research program in science and technology is, nevertheless, a vital component of strategies for countering terrorism and is essential for other, more common problems. No technology can eliminate all vulnerabilities, but prudent application of current knowledge and future research advances in science and technology remains a wise investment.

ROLE OF EPA IN WATER SECURITY

Several federal legislative acts and presidential directives to protect the nation's critical infrastructures against terrorism set out the role of the EPA in coordinating the security of the nation's water systems (see Box 1-1). Within the EPA, both the Office of Water and the Office of Research and Development (ORD) support efforts to carry out these federal laws and directives. This report focuses on the research agenda of the NHSRC within the ORD, but the roles of both EPA offices are briefly described here because both are involved in water and wastewater security.

The Office of Water is responsible for implementing the EPA's water quality activities "including development of national programs, technical policies, and regulations relating to drinking water, water quality, groundwater, pollution source standards, and the protection of wetlands, marine, and estuarine areas."[3] The Office of Water houses the Water Security Division, which provides guidance and tools to drinking water and wastewater utilities as they assess and reduce their vulnerabilities. The Office of Water also provides tools and training to help utilities plan for and practice responses to emergencies, offers technical and financial assistance to utilities to support security initiatives, develops outreach materials, and supports information sharing mechanisms (EPA, 2004a). Additionally, the Office of Water works to develop laboratory capabilities and promote monitoring and detection capacities for drinking water systems under Homeland Security Presidential Directive (HSPD) 9 (see Box 1-1).

The EPA's ORD is the agency's scientific research arm. Its mission is to:

- perform research and development to identify, understand, and solve current and future environmental problems;
- provide responsive technical support to the EPA's mission;
- integrate the work of the ORD's scientific partners (other agencies, nations, private-sector organizations, and academia); and
- provide leadership in addressing emerging environmental issues and in advancing the science and technology of risk assessment and risk management.[4]

The ORD's NHSRC houses the Water Infrastructure Protection Division, which conducts applied research on ways to protect from, mitigate, respond to, and recover from malicious events on water and wastewater systems. Specific examples of the NHSRC's water security initiatives include technical assessments of analytical tools and procedures; evaluations of new technologies; and the development of mathematical models, technical resource databases, decontamination techniques, and risk assessment methods. Most of these research products are intended

---

[3] *http://www.epa.gov/epahome/locate1.htm.*
[4] *http://www.epa.gov/ord/htm/aboutord.htm.*

for use by water security stakeholders, including water and wastewater systems ranging in size from small to large.

The budget of the NHSRC's Water Infrastructure Protection Division was $6 million for each of fiscal years 2005 and 2006 (exclusive of EPA salaries; Kim Fox, EPA, written communication, 2006). This funding level represents a substantial portion of the $16 million available to the entire NHSRC.[5]

Water Security Research and Technical Support Action Plan

In early 2003, a draft Water Security Research and Technical Support Action Plan (Action Plan) was prepared jointly by the ORD and the Office of Water to plan for meeting the EPA's water security responsibilities. The Action Plan covered a three- to four-year time frame (consistent with the envisioned lifespan of the NHSRC, which was established as a "temporary center") and focused on addressing the most immediate water security research and technical support needs. The overall goal was to develop and provide useful tools and technologies to water system managers that would help them protect drinking water and wastewater systems. To achieve this broad goal, the EPA organized the Action Plan and its research projects around the following seven specific issues:

1. protecting drinking water systems from physical and cyber attacks;

2. identifying drinking water threats, contaminants, and other threat scenarios;

3. improving analytical methodologies and monitoring systems for drinking water;

4. containing, treating, decontaminating, and disposing of contaminated water and materials;

5. planning for contingencies and addressing infrastructure interdependencies;

---

[5] The NHSRC focuses its research and development efforts on five primary thrust areas: (1) Threat and Consequence Assessment (improvement of risk assessment techniques), (2) Decontamination & Consequence Management (decontamination of contaminated buildings), (3) Water Infrastructure Protection (protection of U.S. drinking and wastewater systems), (4) Response Capability Enhancement, and (5) Technology Testing and Evaluation (*http://www.epa.gov/nhsrc/about.htm*).

BOX 1-1
Legislative Acts and Directives Set the Context for EPA's Water Security Research Program

Laws and directives germane to the EPA's role in protecting the nation's drinking water and providing related research and technical support include:

- Presidential Decision Directive (PDD) 39: United States Policy on Counterterrorism
- PDD 63: Critical Infrastructure Protection
- Public Health Security and Bioterrorism Preparedness and Response Act (Bioterrorism Act—Public Law No. 107-188),
- National Strategy for Homeland Security (Office of Homeland Security, 2002),
- HSPD-7: Critical Infrastructure Identification, Prioritization, and Protection (Bush, 2003),
- HSPD-9: Defense of United States Agriculture and Food (Bush, 2004), and
- HSPD-10: Biodefense for the 21st Century.[a]

In 1995, the United States Policy on Counterterrorism required all federal agencies to plan for terrorist attacks and designated the EPA to provide environmental response support. In 1998, President Clinton in PDD 63 identified water as one of the nation's critical infrastructures, and the EPA was assigned responsibility as the lead agency for coordinating efforts to protect water from intentional attacks.

The Public Health Security and Bioterrorism Preparedness and Response Act signed in 2002 required the EPA to review: (1) methods to prevent, detect, and respond to the intentional introduction of chemical, biological, or radiological contaminants into community water systems and their source waters and (2) methods by which terrorists or other individuals or groups might disrupt the supply of safe drinking water by interfering with conveyance, collection, treatment, and storage facilities or with cyber infrastructure. It also required the EPA to provide community water systems (those that serve over 3,300 people) with baseline information needed to conduct vulnerability assessments and to provide general security guidance to smaller water systems.

The National Strategy for Homeland Security sought to define the goals of homeland security and the roles of the federal executive branch, nonfederal governments, the privatesector, and citizens in achieving them. Protection of critical infrastructures and key assets is a major thrust. Each critical infrastructure sector is assigned a lead federal agency primarily responsible for coordinating security efforts, and the strategy designated the EPA as the lead agency for the water sector. A Strategic Plan for Homeland Security (EPA, 2002) was subsequently developed to ensure that the EPA met its traditional mission of protecting the environment and safeguarding human health while additionally addressing its new homeland security responsibilities.

HSPD-7 instructs the EPA to take the lead role in protecting the nation's drinking water and wastewater systems. The EPA is accordingly responsible for establishing collaborations among federal departments and agencies, state and local governments, and the private sector. For example, the EPA is responsible for coordinating with the Department of Homeland Security in support of the goals set in the National Infrastructure Protection Plan (DHS, 2006a) for protecting the nation's critical infrastructure. The EPA was also tasked to facilitate the evaluation of vulnerabilities of water systems and to encourage risk management strategies to prevent or mitigate the effects of attacks against critical water infrastructure.

HSPD-9 includes the following tasks for the EPA:

- develop surveillance and monitoring systems for early detection of dangerous agents;
- develop a national laboratory network for water quality;
- enhance intelligence capabilities regarding threats, delivery systems, and methods that could be directed against the water sector;
- create a new capacity to enhance detection and characterization of an attack; and
- expand the development of countermeasures against the intentional introduction or natural occurrence of catastrophic diseases through research on detection methods, prevention technologies, agent characterization, and dose-response relationships for high-consequence agents in the water supply.

HSPD-10 assigns the EPA the responsibility of developing strategies, guidelines, and plans for decontamination, remediation, and cleanup of contamination events, including those involving the water system.

---

[a] See *http://www.fas.org/irp/offdocs/nspd/hspd-10.html* for a nonclassified summary of HSPD-10.

6. targeting impacts on human health and informing the public about risks; and

7. protecting wastewater treatment and collection systems.

The NRC organized a panel of experts and published *A Review of the EPA Water Security Research and Technical Support Action Plan* (NRC, 2004). The report contained recommendations on the research plan and on program strategy, prioritization of research thrusts, leadership, and communication/coordination with stakeholders. While endorsing the EPA's short-term, applied research approach, identification of long-term research needs was also urged.

Following the NRC review, the EPA made revisions to the Action Plan, and additional program adjustments were made as the research program evolved and the NHSRC was made permanent. For example, the NHSRC staff adapted the research plan to respond to recent presidential directives (see Box 1-1). The EPA also sought feedback on its research directions from water and wastewater industry stakeholders through three Water Sector Security Workshops held in 2005 (EPA, 2006c), and the EPA is receiving further guidance on its research program from the Office of Science and Technology Policy and the Department of Homeland Security (DHS).

The work identified in the Action Plan has been conducted in partnership with several water-related professional organizations in the private sector and with other federal agencies. These partners include the American Water Works Association Research Foundation, the Water Environment Research Foundation, the American Society of Civil Engineers, the U.S. Army Corps of Engineers, DHS, the U.S. Army Edgewood Chemical Biological Center, and the National Institute of Standards and Technology. The Action Plan does not attempt to incorporate research and development efforts outside of those funded by the EPA, such as work conducted by private industry.

The products of the Action Plan to date have largely focused upon making compilations of existing data available to water infrastructure customers through various media (e.g., documents, online databases, training modules). The NHSRC also conducts applied research to address data gaps and develop new methods and tools, but the practical needs of water infrastructure stakeholders remain the driving force behind all of these initiatives. The importance of the NHSRC's technical support role is not only evident from these activities but also from the following statement of the NHSRC goals for fiscal year 2005:

- to focus on technical information exchange and collaborations with the water industry, addressing the needs outlined in the Action Plan, and to continue to work with the DHS and other partners;
- to revisit issues and needs with key stakeholder and user groups;
- to communicate results of EPA research and technical support under the Action Plan; and
- to introduce and test products for use by stakeholders (J. Herrmann, EPA, personal communication, 2005).

COMMITTEE CHARGE

Following the first NRC review, the EPA again approached the NRC for advice on its water security research program. The EPA was approaching the end of the planning time frames originally developed in the Action Plan, and this second NRC study was motivated in large part by the shift in status of the NHSRC from temporary to permanent and the accompanying need to address strategic planning for long-term research. The NRC's Water Science and Technology Board appointed a committee of experts that was tasked to:

1. provide a readily accessible cadre of experience, knowledge, and expertise to advise EPA in support of efforts to maintain safety of the nation's water supplies and wastewater systems;
2. review progress by the EPA on its water security activities, including the Water Security Research and Technical Support Action Plan;
3. identify and prioritize short- and long-term research needs in the area of water security, highlighting opportunities for the EPA and other federal and state agencies; and
4. identify opportunities for coordination of water-security-related research and improved communication of the results with relevant entities.

To address its task, the committee held five meetings between January 2005 and May 2006. The committee examined relevant EPA documents (both public and classified documents) that had been published by May 2006 and related scientific literature. The committee also received briefings at its public meetings from EPA staff and other organizations and individuals involved in water security research, received classified briefings with EPA staff, and conducted a site visit to the EPA's water security research facilities. The review of EPA's progress on the Action Plan was limited because only a small fraction of the total number of intended products had been published by May 2006. Therefore, much of the review of progress was based on oral and written progress reports (e.g., EPA, 2005a) provided by EPA staff. The committee was also unable to review in detail some of the EPA's ongoing water security work, such as the Water Sentinel program, because sensitive but unclassified security information could not be protected within NRC operating procedures under Section 15 of the Federal Advisory Committee Act. The committee issued a letter report in November 2005, highlighting immediate opportunities for water security research in the aftermath of Hurricane Katrina (NRC, 2005; see Appendix A).

In this, the committee's final report, the committee evaluates research progress to date, analyzes lessons learned from the first four years, and looks ahead to a vision of EPA's water security research program with specific recommendations for strengthening it. The report is presented in six chapters. Challenges to the EPA in the implementation of its water security research program are discussed in Chapter 2. The committee presents its approach to this study, including criteria for evaluating the value and priority of the EPA water security projects, in Chapter 3. The committee's assessment of the EPA's research progress is presented in Chapter 4. Recommendations for improving program implementation and research management are provided in Chapter 5. Recommendations for future research, including ways to address key gaps in the current research program, are discussed in Chapter 6.

2

EPA's Challenges in Water Security Research

The Environmental Protection Agency (EPA) has been engaged in water security research for four years, and research management and technical issues specific to water security both guide and constrain its activities. A review of the EPA's research efforts and suggestions for future research and programmatic directions (discussed in Chapters 4, 5, and 6) requires recognition of these challenges as important context for this report.

TECHNICAL CHALLENGES

The technical challenges facing the EPA water security research program are defined by the diversity and size of the water and wastewater sectors and the rapid evolution of water security research information.

Diversity and Number of Water and Wastewater Systems

The task of designing a research program that ultimately improves the security and response capabilities of the nation's water or wastewater sector would be sufficiently challenging if only one or a few such systems needed to be protected. However, the nation's "drinking water system" is in reality a large number of heterogeneous and separate systems, ranging in size from 15 connections up to many millions. While EPA regulations produce some technological commonalities, tremendous variety exists. The EPA estimates that the United States has some 160,000 public drinking water systems, each supplying at least 25 persons or 15 service connections on a regular basis (EPA, 2004c). About one-third of this total number (53,000) are "community water systems," which serve cities, towns, mobile home parks, or residential developments. Most community systems are quite small, with 84 percent serving fewer than 3,300 persons each. "Noncommunity systems" are usually smaller, supplying individual schools, factories, campgrounds, or hotels, for example. The EPA estimates that about 107,000 noncommunity systems exist in the United States, although in aggregate, these small systems supply less than 10 percent of the U.S. population. Drinking water sources are also varied, from large surface water impoundments (reservoirs) or natural surface water bodies (e.g., lakes, rivers) to groundwater systems served by aquifers of varying complexity, interconnectedness, depth, and physical characteristics.

The municipal wastewater industry has over 16,000 plants that are used to treat a total flow on the order of 32,000 billion gallons per day (Bgal/d). More than 92 percent of the total existing flow is handled by about 3,000 treatment plants that have a treatment capacity of 1 million gallons per day (Mgal/d) or greater, although more than 6,000 plants treat a flow of 100,000 gallons per day or less (EPA, 1997). Nearly all of the wastewater treatment plants provide some form of secondary treatment and more than half provide some form of advanced treatment using a diversity of treatment processes and configurations. Thus, crafting a wastewater security research strategy that is suitable for all wastewater treatment plants is difficult.

Protecting a very large number of utilities against the consequences of the wide range of possible threats is a daunting, perhaps impossible, task. The development of a workable security system to prevent physical attacks against commercial airline flights is difficult and is still a work in progress, and the comparable problem for water systems is vastly more complex. Security technologies for one type of system might not work for another, and many systems might require custom designs. Further, no systems are immune from concern about an attack. A chemical or biological attack on a system that serves only a few thousand people would still be significant in terms of loss of life, economic damage, or the amount of fear and loss of confidence it would cause. In addition, smaller systems tend to be less protected and more vulnerable to a malicious attack. Approximately 160,000 drinking water systems and 16,000 wastewater systems operate simultaneously 24 hours a day, 7 days a week, with the largest systems each servicing millions of customers, and each is capable of being attacked by many different means requiring different methods of prevention. Expecting utilities to harden water and wastewater infrastructure to eliminate all vulnerabilities is unreasonable. The costs of security for the industry would be borne by the end users, and these users may not be willing to bear the costs of developing and implementing technologies that could prevent even a limited range of terrorist attacks over the entire nation's water and wastewater systems.

The diversity and number of water and wastewater systems pose specific problems for the development of workable and sustainable security technologies, such as chemical and biological agent detection and disease surveillance technology, which need to be considered in the development of a water security research agenda. These issues are discussed in detail below.

Challenges for Detection Technology

In most sectors, early detection is regarded as important to prevent or minimize damage from an intentional contamination attack. The detection might theoretically occur prior to any exposure, enabling preventive actions ("detect to protect") or warnings to potential end users ("detect to warn"). Detection might also occur after exposure has occurred, possibly supplying sufficiently timely information to encourage exposed persons to seek appropriate treatment ("detect to treat"). Clearly, the earlier a contaminant is detected, the greater the likelihood that its public health impact can be reduced. Thus, an initial research interest has focused on developing early detection systems for chemical or biological agents that might intentionally be introduced into water or wastewater. Any such effort, however, will have to overcome some significant challenges to fashion advanced technologies into a workable system, considering the challenge of the number and diversity of water and wastewater systems and potential contaminants.

The problem can be reduced to a matter of simple arithmetic. Every detector balances the ability to detect even the smallest and most transient of signals (i.e., sensitivity) against the need to avoid setting off an alarm erroneously. Ideally, extremely high sensitivity should be paired with an extraordinarily low false positive rate. However, even if the probability of attack on *some* water system were relatively high, the probability of attack on any *particular* one of the 160,000 water systems is still very low. Let us assume, for example, a very high rate of one such intentional attack per year among the largest 10,000 drinking water systems. To detect such an attack, sensors would have to be placed throughout the systems and take frequent measurements. If a generic intrusion detector samples once every 10 minutes and there are on average 20 detectors per system (a reasonable assumption for one of the 10,000 largest systems, although one might expect more for a very large system and fewer for a very small system), this adds up to a million sampling intervals per system per year. Assuming a false positive rate of one in 10 million measurements (an extraordinarily small rate if also maximizing sensitivity), this would still produce 1,000 false positives per year among these 10,000 water systems. If only one true positive in 10,000 is expected, this means that almost every time the alarm goes off (99.9 percent of the time), it is a false positive.[1] As a result, operators are likely to disconnect, ignore, or simply choose not to install the detection system. If detectors are ignored or not maintained, they cannot practically serve their purpose, whether to prevent, warn, or treat.

The problem is compounded when considering the installation of detectors for each of a large number of potential biothreat agents. Meinhardt (2005) published a table of 28 *selected* agents in 8 broad categories identified by multiple governmental, military, and medical sources as possible biowarfare agents that might present a public health threat if dispersed by water. Assuming success in constructing a 100 percent sensitive and extremely specific detector for the eight broad agent categories (e.g., viral pathogen, marine biotoxin) and assuming each broad category has an equal probability of being employed in an attack, the probability of a true alarm is reduced by almost another order of magnitude. In other words, the additional analysis of multiple categories of agents requires an order-of-magnitude reduction in the false positive rate of a detector just to get back to the unsatisfactory baseline of a system for a generic intrusion detector.

The fundamental problem relates to the rarity of an attack on any particular system. Detectors can be made with high sensitivity and specificity (low false positive and false negative rates), but when applied in situations where the event to be detected is uncommon, the predictive value of an alarm can be very small. Positive predictive value is defined as the number of true positives divided by the total number of positive results (including both true and false positives). This predictive measure is improved if the likelihood of an event is higher.

A false positive alarm every few years might conceivably be acceptable to some communities that consider themselves high-risk targets, assuming there is an agreed-upon response plan in place for a positive signal. An acceptable community response plan, which would include a protocol for confirmatory testing and public notification, requires joint

---

[1] The calculations were conducted as follows:
10,000 water systems * 20 detectors/system * 6 measurements/detector/hour * 8760 hours/year = 10,512,000,000 measurements/year across all 10,000 systems. Given the assumptions in this scenario of a false positive rate of one in 10 million measurements and an attack rate of one per 10,000 drinking water systems, there will be approximately 1,000 false positives and only one is a true positive (one attack) per year.

agreement between utility, health department, first responders, and politicians. Rigorous industry-wide employee training would be required to ensure timely response after a positive alarm.

These challenges have practical implications for the EPA's research program. Contaminant monitoring systems aim to detect a low-probability, high-consequence event. Therefore, suitable instruments need to be highly sensitive and specific for the agents they are intended to detect and ideally should be very low maintenance. Improved event detection architecture could possibly reduce the number of false positives. In this approach, a water system would install an array of sensors linked in a way that only triggers an alarm when a statistically significant number of sensors detect abnormal levels. This should reduce or eliminate the false positives caused by independent sensor malfunctions, but it would also increase the false negative rate (i.e., decrease specificity) and the cost of the detection system. The cost of purchasing and maintaining such detection instruments over a period of years needs to be considered in evaluating the likelihood of implementation. These sizeable technology requirements suggest that contaminant detection devices with a reasonable likelihood of widespread implementation and successful operation (even in a detect to treat capacity) remain a challenging long-term research goal. Research suggestions related to contaminant detection systems are discussed further in Chapter 6.

Challenges for Disease Surveillance Systems

Disease surveillance systems have been proposed as another method to detect a drinking water contamination event (Berger et al., 2006; Buehler et al., 2003; CDC, 2003a; 2006). The detection of a water-related event using a human-disease-based surveillance system with an appropriate epidemiologic follow-up investigation is insensitive to any but the largest outbreak events and would occur too late to prevent illness. However, disease surveillance systems could be used to mitigate further exposure and implement treatment or prophylaxis (detect to treat), especially if linked to contaminant monitoring systems.

The problems associated with *in situ* detection systems, discussed in the previous section, apply with even more force to disease surveillance systems designed to detect specific syndromes related to bioterror agents, because disease surveillance systems have only modest sensitivities and specificities. The body's immune system reacts generically to many infections in their initial stages to produce the ubiquitous "flu-like symptoms" seen in so many different diseases at first presentation.

The implementation of enhanced disease surveillance systems is costly and has inherent false positive and negative rates. For example, not every case of waterborne disease will eventually be diagnosed as such. Therefore it has been argued (Stoto et al., 2004) that the benefits of such enhanced systems may not outweigh the costs in the general case. Public health researchers have argued that "it is challenging to develop sensible response protocols for syndromic surveillance systems because the likelihood of false alarms is so high, and because information is currently not specific enough to enable more timely outbreak detection or disease control activities" (Berger et al., 2006). Furthermore, implementation of a disease surveillance system for homeland security concerns alone would be difficult to maintain based on the overall likelihood of an event and the large number of utilities at risk.

Rapid Evolution of Scientific Information Relevant to Water Security

Since September 11, 2001, the federal government has substantially increased funding directed toward homeland security-related research, including research on biothreat agents (Altman et al., 2005). Although much of the research pertinent to water security is still in progress, the amount of scientific information has increased substantially, and this surge of information is expected to continue in the years ahead. Thus, current researchers and research managers will be hard pressed to stay abreast of the advances in technology and new information regarding specific agents, especially considering the additional security concerns that keep much of the new information out of the scientific literature.

The volume of scientific information from a wide variety of fields that bear on the subject of water security (e.g., engineering, molecular biology, environmental science, social science) is also large and difficult to integrate. The subject matter is more than multidisciplinary but interdisciplinary. Researchers from disparate disciplines cannot simply work separately on the same problems but need to cross disciplines and consider problems in unaccustomed ways. Water security researchers also need to use information from fields far from their disciplinary home territories. The value of interdisciplinary approaches to complex scientific and technical problems is now well recognized, although educational and institutional structures have been slow to adapt. Not only do technical details and knowledge vary among disciplines, but attitudes, approaches, and language vary as well, sometimes leading to unrecognized difficulties in communication (Keller, 2002). These interdisciplinary challenges are complicated further with the addition of the social sciences. The problem of terrorism involves social science questions in a fundamental way (e.g., How will people respond in a time of crisis? How can water security risks be effectively communicated to the public?), and the social sciences cannot and should not be neglected even in setting what appears to be a purely technical research agenda (see Chapter 6).

CHALLENGES FOR RESEARCH MANAGEMENT

The EPA faces multiple research management challenges in its water security program. These challenges include the difficulties of interdisciplinary and interagency coordination, assuring stable leadership, balancing short-term and long-term research initiatives, allowing information sharing in the context of national security, balancing the needs of multiple constituencies, and building sufficient staff expertise.

Interdisciplinary and Interagency Coordination

Managing an interdisciplinary research program requires integrating a variety of disciplines that normally have not worked together and meeting the needs of each. The challenge is compounded for the EPA's National Homeland Security Research Center (NHSRC) by the need to coordinate with different offices and divisions within EPA, numerous trade associations, and other federal and state agencies that may have overlapping and sometimes ambiguous jurisdictions. The challenge is well illustrated by the recent confusion as to which federal cabinet department would be the lead agency in the event of a pandemic from avian influenza. Both the Department of Homeland Security (DHS) and the Department of Health and Human Services claimed lead status, each citing the same National Response Plan and associated presidential directives as justification (Nesmith and McKenna, 2005).

External mandates from presidential directives or requests from the DHS are unpredictable management constraints, independent of a planned research agenda, but cannot be ignored. Sometimes such mandates are sufficiently vague as to allow flexibility, but vague mandates can also cause confusion as agency managers may interpret them differently.

Stable Leadership

Frequent shifts in management personnel have become commonplace in federal service and represent a particular challenge to managing a long-term research agenda. Shifting demands and resources also put pressure on the desirable goal of continuity in management and personnel. Two possible consequences are a constantly shifting set of new goals and objectives or the ossification of an original and possibly out-of-date set of goals and objectives. Moreover, flexibility and adaptation require some kind of institutional memory and perspective, which is particularly difficult in the face of continual changes in management. This issue was raised in the National Research Council's review of the EPA Action Plan (NRC, 2004), and so far, the changes that have occurred in the EPA's water security research management have maintained good institutional continuity. Nevertheless, these management issues should be recognized as they will likely continue to raise serious challenges for implementing a long-term research agenda.

Pressure for Rapid Results versus Long-Term Strategies

Research agendas have inherent time scales, which can be roughly categorized as short-term (less than two years), medium-term (two to five years) and long-term (longer than five years). The EPA's initial efforts in water security research and technical support appropriately emphasized the most urgent questions that could be addressed within a three- to four-year time frame, but now the agency is looking toward building a balance of short-term and longer-term research.

As events evolve, there are pressures to turn research management attention from one area to another. Management pressures are often focused on the most immediate, urgent, and shortest-term questions. Sometimes those pressures are appropriate, but often they are the product of the moment. If efforts are expended continually in responding to immediate concerns, resources are reduced for the more sustained efforts that a mid- to long-term research agenda requires. Some of the continuing pressure toward short-term research comes from the interaction of newly developed information and external mandates. The result of such pressures can be a constantly shifting focus of attention, with a concomitant underresourcing of the mid- and longer-term efforts. Although understandable, the continual shifting focus presents a genuine management dilemma—a challenge that requires stable management if it is to be met.

Information Sharing in the Context of National Security

Balancing information security concerns versus operational need-to-know and the benefits of scientific and technical information sharing is among the most significant challenges in water security research management, especially as response time will be critical in minimizing consequences. Open exchange of information is preferred, where feasible, because it allows the most efficient progress to be made in solving difficult problems. The more people working on a complicated problem, the more likely that an innovative solution will be found. Yet, there is a widespread concern that some kinds of information cannot be shared, even with end users, because the information has the potential to be used in a way that might be harmful.

The EPA faces risks in providing water security information and risks in withholding it, and there is no easy solution to a problem that involves risks on both sides. As an example, if research were to find an unforeseen but easy way to contaminate a system, this information might change how utilities protect themselves and improve their ability to recognize that an attack has taken place. At the same time, this information can be used for malicious purposes. As a result, there is a delicate balance between alerting a significant number of water operators of a danger, while minimizing the potential for suggesting a route of attack to a malefactor. Current approaches for distributing water security research information in a more secure manner to a limited number of people are described in Box 2-1.

Multiple Constituencies

The EPA has to be responsive to at least four separate constituencies with different needs and concerns: (1) DHS and cognate agencies with responsibility for national security; (2) the water industry; (3) state and local agencies involved with preparedness, emergency response, and environmental regulation; and (4) the public. Concerns about information

BOX 2-1
Mechanisms for Disseminating Homeland Security Information

The Water Information Sharing and Analysis Center (WaterISAC) was established as an outcome of Presidential Decision Directive 63 (see Box 1-1), calling for the establishment of ISACs for the sharing of security and sector-sensitive information within the private sector and with the federal government. The WaterISAC is a subscription-based service open to all drinking water and wastewater utilities within the United States, regardless of the size of the population served or the ownership. State administrators as well as certain EPA personnel also have access. The WaterISAC currently reaches 1,020 individuals at 512 water utilities that provide water services to 65 percent of the American population (D. VanDe Hei, WaterISAC, personal communication, 2006).

The Water Security Channel (WaterSC) is managed by the WaterISAC and is designed to reach the drinking water and wastewater utilities that have not subscribed to the more comprehensive services of the WaterISAC. The WaterSC reaches 9,558 individuals at 8,447 organizations (D. VanDe Hei, WaterISAC, personal communication, 2006). WaterSC affiliates include utilities as well as state primacy organizations, government organizations, engineering firms, and researchers. The services of the WaterSC are free and available to all utilities and organizations concerned with water security. Both the WaterISAC and the WaterSC are partially funded through an EPA grant.

WaterISAC and WaterSC security protocols require users to be authenticated before accepting and authorizing access to information. Because the WaterISAC handles highly sensitive information, its vetting

---

sharing exemplify the challenge of multiple constituencies that the EPA faces in its water security research program. Federal agencies responsible for homeland security favor restrictions on information sharing to minimize potential risks. The water industry and state and local agencies need readily available information and tools that can be implemented practically and routinely, although the particulars can vary widely among utilities. The public needs enough information to have confidence in the safety of the water supply, the means to protect themselves in the event of an attack, and the ability to determine and understand when the supply is safe again.

Adding to the complexity of these multiple constituencies, the water and wastewater industry is not only heterogeneous in size but also in ownership and management, with a mixture of public, private, and public-private models. The EPA, therefore, works with a variety of trade

process is more rigorous. The WaterISAC also has a double authentication protocol in place to ensure that only authorized individuals access a designated document.

When new and urgent information becomes available, WaterISAC and WaterSC participants are informed via e-mail and online notification databases. Participants can also be notified by text messages directly to their cell phones. The water-sector individual is informed of the location of the information including a link to its contents and a brief overview so that the individual can determine if the document would be of use in the particular circumstance. Additionally, WaterISAC and WaterSC Web sites host newly released information in file format. The Water Sector Coordinating Council (WSCC), a group representing the water sector that was organized to give advice to DHS, has recognized the WaterISAC, including its supplementary WaterSC, as the primary communication tool within the water sector (L. Stovall, Chair, WSCC, personal communication, 2006).

An additional communication software platform exists in the Homeland Security Information Network (HSIN), which was launched by the DHS as a communications tool to make federal information available to a broad range of U.S. businesses and individuals. The HSIN is being offered to all critical infrastructure sectors, including the water sector. Because of the vast audience, sensitive data cannot be made available on the HSIN, as it can be on the WaterISAC. After an evaluation of the HSIN's capabilities, a recommendation to integrate the HSIN into the suite of communication tools used by the WaterISAC was made and approved by both the WaterISAC Board and the WSCC. The HSIN, as well as the WaterSC, will be available at no cost to all utilities, state primacy organizations, government organizations, engineering firms, researchers, and other interested parties.

associations and other interest groups (e.g., those representing rural water systems, municipal systems, investor-owned systems), each of which has its own set of incentives, disincentives, constraints, and relative financial sensitivities for various kinds of security investments and objectives. Research on protective methods might be directed differently if it were aimed at optimizing personnel costs, capital costs, maintenance costs, water rates, or some particular mixture of these. Thus, research products are of differential use to small or large systems, to urban or rural, or to those in certain competitive or public-sector financing environments. Decisions about a research agenda often do not explicitly acknowledge these differences, which are only recognized later if a significant sector of the industry has not been taken into account.

Negotiating a research agenda through contradictory needs and constraints presented by such a heterogeneous industry and these multiple constituencies is a significant challenge. Research priorities may be more or less tailored to any or all of these constituencies, although institutional pressures may favor the needs of cognate agencies within the federal government.

The usefulness of the EPA's research agenda, however, will depend upon meeting the needs of the industry, and its ultimate success rests upon meeting the needs of the public.

EPA's Roles and Capabilities

If the EPA's water security research tasks combined with the above management issues were to be considered *de novo*, it would be an enormous challenge, but the tasks have been imposed on existing agency structure and expertise. The EPA cannot start afresh and is expected to use existing strengths and address gaps in a variety of ways.

Today, the EPA is primarily a regulatory agency, not a research agency. Its strengths have traditionally related to understanding and controlling environmental and public health risks, including contamination, operational details of regulations, and cost-benefit assessments of proposed requirements. The Office of Research and Development (ORD) research facility in Cincinnati, where the NHSRC is housed, is an exception. The skills of the ORD and specifically the NHSRC have evolved to complement the regulatory portfolio of the agency as a whole, although many of these skills remain useful for large portions of the water security research portfolio. The agency's regulatory emphasis, however, has shaped the current staff expertise, and several conspicuous gaps now exist within the NHSRC's water security program. For example, the EPA lacks subject matter experts in issues such as cyber security and explosive attacks. Additionally, the EPA is only now beginning to acquire expertise in the social sciences needed for understanding public reaction to water security incidents, how information and misinformation spreads, and how to communicate effectively with the public and public officials. The EPA has recognized many of these weaknesses and has entered into research partnerships with the U.S. Army Corps of Engineers and other relevant agencies to obtain complementary expertise. Outside contracting, however, requires significant agency oversight to ensure the projects are planned and carried out in a way that best supports the needs of key stakeholders, including the water and wastewater industry.

The EPA has been handed a task that is new to its historic mission, expertise, and mindset. Not unexpectedly in these fiscally austere times, it has also been asked to accomplish the task with relatively modest resources. A long-term water security research agenda could easily be envisioned that would require several times the budget of the EPA's current program. Because such funding is not likely or reasonable considering the agency's other obligations, a framework for evaluating and prioritizing the water security research enterprise is necessary for making the inevitable choices. The committee's approach and general prioritizing criteria that shape its recommendations are presented in Chapter 3.

SUMMARY

The many challenges faced by the EPA's water security program as it moves beyond the targeted short-term research and technical support objectives of the Action Plan are outlined in this chapter. These challenges range from the inherently technical to the managerial. The number and diversity of water and wastewater systems, for example, creates challenges for crafting a research agenda that is responsive to the needs of end users and also creates specific challenges for the development of water security technologies. Challenges for research management include the problems of multiple constituencies and disparate outside forces that constrain and sometimes redirect efforts. The EPA also faces challenges with information sharing and building a research program considering existing programmatic strengths and weaknesses. These challenges provide an important context for the findings and recommendations that follow.

3

Committee's Approach

The criteria used by the committee to frame its review of progress of the Water Security Research and Technical Support Action Plan (Action Plan) and to guide recommendations for a long-term water security research program (see statement of task, Chapter 1) are presented in this chapter. The committee's organizing assumptions and strategic criteria for future research management decisions, like its evaluations of the Action Plan, were framed from the perspective of the challenges and constraints outlined in Chapter 2.

The committee's criteria are premised upon several broad findings. First, the Environmental Protection Agency's (EPA's) Office of Research and Development is working within a limited budget, and water security research cannot replace other essential research to support public health and the needs of water and wastewater utilities. Second, preventing a terrorist attack on the nation's water infrastructure may be impossible because of the number and diversity of utilities, the multiple points of vulnerability, and the expense of protecting an entire system. Thus, the committee focused its attention on research to prevent or mitigate the *consequences* of an attack or attempted attack. Third, the information and technical products of the water security research program will be most valuable if they have dual-use benefits. For this report, "dual use" refers to research on technologies that addresses both security and important water utility objectives. Examples include identifying security measures that can mitigate the effects of both physical attacks and earthquake hazards or developing a water quality detection system that can be used to detect generic intrusion events while also providing data on key water quality parameters used to monitor system operations. Dual use can also apply to information technologies (e.g., databases) and their use for natural or accidental contamination events in addition to terrorist threats. In the committee's usage, dual use was not meant to include work that addresses more than one purpose within homeland security (e.g., measures that safeguard both water and food from a biothreat agent attack).

From the findings described above, the committee identified four criteria to guide its evaluation of the value of the EPA's water security research projects and to provide a foundation for its recommendations for future research priorities:

1. Water security threats with the greatest likelihood and potential consequences (including fatalities, sickness, economic losses, and loss of public confidence) are addressed.

2. Effectiveness and efficiency of the nation's response and recovery capacity are improved, and/or risk reduction or consequence mitigation measures are developed.

3. Implementation of new technologies/methodologies is judged to be likely, taking into account their cost, usefulness, and maintenance requirements.

4. Dual-use benefits accrue from the research.

Dual-use benefits are included among these criteria because they significantly improve the likelihood of implementation of the research products, and there is strong support for research with dual-use applications within the water industry and the public. Research in support of improved mitigation, recovery, and response is often of dual use because it can be applied to address both natural hazards and terrorist events. However, the committee does not view dual use as an absolute requirement for all water security research. These criteria shape the committee's evaluations and recommendations in Chapters 4 through 6.

These criteria could also be used at a later date to evaluate the effectiveness and success of the program, although such an evaluation was not feasible here based on the number of products available at the time of the committee's review. In sum, water security risks should be reduced if research products can be shown to address probable threats with significant consequences and if utilities or local, state, and federal response agencies use these products to address security vulnerabilities or to improve the effectiveness of response and recovery.

4

Progress in the Office of Research and Development's Water Security Program

When the Environmental Protection Agency (EPA) established the National Homeland Security Research Center (NHSRC) in 2002 as a temporary center with a lifespan of three years, the Water Security Research and Technical Support Action Plan (Action Plan) provided a framework for identifying projects that could make timely and functional contributions to water security needs. The progress that has been made on the Action Plan by May 2006 is described in this chapter, along with some of the most significant products, tools, and guidance that have been developed out of the research program. The purpose of this chapter is to evaluate this work relative to the criteria described in Chapter 3. Because only a small percentage of the anticipated research products had been released during the committee's review, the effectiveness of the program—that is, whether the information and data developed by the NHSRC are being used to reduce water security risks—could not be usefully evaluated. The committee based much of its analysis on information gained through discussions with EPA staff or its contractors. A critique directed at each of the Action Plan projects is neither within the scope of the committee's charge nor possible without more detailed information than provided thus far by the EPA. Based on the evaluations in this chapter, recommendations for improving research management and priorities for future short- and long-term research are presented in Chapters 5 and 6, respectively.

The committee's review of the EPA water security research program is organized below according to the original Action Plan research categories:

1. protecting drinking water systems from physical and cyber attacks;
2. identifying drinking water threats, contaminants, and other threat scenarios;

3. improving analytical methodologies and monitoring systems for drinking water;

4. containing, treating, decontaminating, and disposing of contaminated water and materials;

5. planning for contingencies and addressing infrastructure interdependencies;

6. targeting impacts on human health and informing the public about risks; and

7. protecting wastewater treatment and collection systems.

In each category, the discussions of progress and continued needs have been further organized in terms of advances in knowledge, new analytical tools, and the development of guidance, protocols, and training, as appropriate. The EPA's technology testing and research communication strategies are also discussed in this chapter.

PROTECTING DRINKING WATER SYSTEMS FROM PHYSICAL AND CYBER THREATS (ACTION PLAN SECTION 3.1)

In Section 3.1 of the Action Plan, the EPA identified priority research and technical support on the topic of physical and cyber security in three areas:

3.1.a. Identification and prioritization of physical and cyber security threats,

3.1.b. Understanding the consequences for water systems from physical and cyber attacks, and

3.1.c. Designing countermeasures for preventing or mitigating the effects of physical or cyber attacks.

The Action Plan (EPA, 2004a) described eight projects to address these issues, emphasizing blast effects as one of the most likely methods employed by terrorists. Cyber security is also addressed, although the work focuses on applying lessons learned from other industries to the water sector. Out of nine products that are planned from this work, four products[1] had been produced as of May 2006 (e.g., ASCE et al., 2004a; EPA, 2004b), focusing on vulnerability assessment methodologies and interim design guidance to improve security. One tool for assessing the consequences of physical attacks (AT Planner) was also undergoing preliminary testing (see EPA, 2005a).

Advances in Knowledge

Security risks are a function of the likelihood of threats, potential consequences, and local vulnerabilities. The EPA and utility managers are well aware of water system vulnerabilities now that most mid- and large-sized utilities have completed vulnerability assessments, but information on threats and consequences remains incomplete. In a classified report, the EPA identified and ranked the most likely intentional contamination threats to drinking water using a risk-based method taking into account feasibility, availability of materials, and public health, economic, and environmental impacts (EPA, 2004b). However, as yet, a threat and consequence analysis of physical and cyber threat scenarios for water systems comparable to the analysis of biological and contamination threats does not seem to be available, even though numerous physical and cyber threat scenarios can be envisioned that could cause major service disruptions or flooding. Lack of EPA expertise in both the cyber and physical attack areas may be affecting more thorough analysis in these areas. Utilities need information on the threats and consequences of physical, cyber, and contaminant attacks to assess their security risks and to provide adequate justification to decision makers on any warranted security upgrades or consequence mitigation measures. The EPA also needs this information to set priorities for its own research efforts.

New Analytical Tools

The EPA is collaborating with the U.S. Army Corps of Engineers' (USACE) Engineering Research and Development Center (ERDC) to develop a software tool—AT Planner—that can be used to estimate blast

---

[1] For the purpose of this report, research products reflect those tools, reports, and substantive research articles identified in EPA (2005a) as published or planned outcomes of the Action Plan efforts.

damage to water or wastewater facilities. The tool will be useful for utilities to estimate standoff distances and to evaluate the expected performance of planned security upgrades so that utilities can evaluate ways to reduce risk or mitigate the consequences of an attack. The software includes preliminary recommendations for facility hardening and redundancy options and provides recommendations for actions to enhance recovery. AT Planner is currently under evaluation by the EPA and select water utility operators.

The Action Plan effort contributed to the refinement of two methodologies for conducting vulnerability assessments at water and wastewater utilities: the Risk Assessment Methodology for Water Utilities (RAM-W) and the Vulnerability Self Assessment Tool (VSAT). These are valuable tools to assess vulnerabilities at individual utilities, so that utility managers can take steps to manage their risks. However, these existing tools for risk assessment do not contain all of the elements for a complete risk management approach. This topic is addressed further in Chapter 6.

Development of Guidance, Protocols, and Training

Interim voluntary design standards to improve security at water and wastewater utilities have been developed (ASCE et al., 2004a; 2004b) that offer useful guidance both for security and nonsecurity purposes (dual use). However, the design standards are specific to existing system designs and do not consider visionary designs for future water systems that could both optimize operations while reducing security concerns.

The American Water Works Association Research Foundation (AwwaRF) and the Water Environment Research Foundation (WERF) are developing a guidance document to address cyber security at drinking water and wastewater utilities, applying lessons learned from other critical infrastructure sectors. Considering the importance of supervisory control and data acquisition (SCADA) systems to daily operations at many large utilities, this project is critical to improving security for water systems.

Following a recommendation in NRC (2004), the EPA has established a Web site[2] describing the costs and benefits of various security products that address physical, cyber, and/or contaminant threats. The

---

[2] *http://cfpub.epa.gov/safewater/watersecurity/guide/.*

Web site also provides links to technology testing data from the Environmental Technology Verification program and the Technology Testing and Evaluation Program, described later in this chapter. This Web site provides useful guidance to utility managers as they assess alternatives available for improving security. However, the risk reduction benefits of security measures need to be carefully considered in the context of other consequence mitigation options, including recovery strategies, early warning and evacuation, emergency action planning, and contingency planning.

Training with industry for blast vulnerability assessment has been initiated on a limited basis using AT Planner, and additional training workshops are anticipated nationwide. This interim training/evaluation process will assist the EPA in determining whether AT Planner meets the needs of the water managers when it is eventually deployed to the owners.

Assessment

Overall, the EPA efforts in physical and cyber security are limited in scope, reflecting the relatively low priority of the topic to the EPA. The committee is concerned that the potential seriousness of physical attacks on a drinking water system are being overlooked, and therefore, contingencies and recovery options for physical attacks are not being addressed adequately in the research agenda. The lack of in-house expertise on the topics of physical and cyber security further limits the EPA's ability to take a leadership role in this area, because contract management alone offers limited guidance and oversight to the work being performed. Nevertheless, the EPA has made significant progress on some key projects in this area (e.g., AT Planner).

IDENTIFYING DRINKING WATER THREATS, CONTAMINANTS, AND THREAT SCENARIOS (ACTION PLAN SECTION 3.2)

Priority items for the EPA to accomplish in the area of identifying drinking water contaminants are listed in Section 3.2 of the Action Plan. This section is divided into four areas:

3.2.a.   A manageable, prioritized list of threats, contaminants, and threat scenarios for drinking water supplies and systems;

3.2.b.   A contaminant identification tool that describes critically important information on contaminants with the potential to harm drinking water supplies and systems;

3.2.c.   A set of carefully selected surrogates or simulants for use in testing and evaluating fate and transport characteristics and treatment technologies for priority contaminants; and

3.2.d.   Methods and means to securely maintain and transmit information on threats, contaminants, and threat scenarios applicable to drinking water supplies and systems.

To address these issues, 10 projects were identified in the EPA Action Plan (see EPA, 2004a).   As of May 2006, notable progress had been made in the first two subsets; a prioritized list of contaminants and a contaminant database had been produced from this work.   Research on surrogates (3.2.c) is under way, and   three additional products were anticipated, including training modules and improvements to the database (see EPA, 2005a).

Advances in Knowledge

The EPA is collaborating with other organizations to develop a set of carefully selected surrogates or simulants.   For example, the EPA is working with the U.S. Army's Edgewood Chemical Biological Center (Edgewood) to identify surrogates and simulants for six priority biological warfare agents (four bacteria and two biotoxins) and to identify or develop methods for detecting those surrogates using molecular identification procedures.   Edgewood will also examine the fate and transport characteristics of the surrogates and the disinfection effectiveness of chlorine and chloramination for inactivating those surrogates.   The EPA and Edgewood have recently signed an agreement to carry out similar work for one virus.   The EPA is also working with the Centers for Disease Control and Prevention (CDC) on a similar surrogate project for anthrax (EPA, 2006d; Rice et al., 2005; Rose et al., 2005).   The availability of surrogate organisms for highly pathogenic select agents (e.g., some microorganisms, biotoxins) could greatly facilitate and broaden research that is relevant to homeland security as well as to academia and industry.   Use of attenuated or avirulent strains or organisms that are taxonomically related to pathogens generally reduces the laboratory biosafety and regulatory requirements associated with select agent work. However, from the experience to date, it appears that one surrogate per pathogen is not adequate to address all research needs. Work related to the identification of *Bacillus anthracis* surrogates, although not of highest priority for water security, still provides a good example of some of the difficulties and time investments required to identify suitable surrogates (see Box 4-1).

Whether a surrogate is needed that matches *closely* or *broadly* the pathogen characteristics of interest is a critical question. The answer depends on the type of research question to be addressed with the surrogate. Surrogates that broadly reflect properties of a select agent or that represent the "upper bounds" or "worst case" properties of a select agent also may be useful in some types of research. For example, viral surrogates for SARS, avian flu virus, and hemorrhagic fever viruses would be useful for studying issues related to fate, transport, and disinfection of these types of viruses in drinking and wastewater. Since these viruses all have a lipid envelope, and since such envelopes can affect environmental fate and transport characteristics, initial studies could be completed rapidly if a nonpathogenic, surrogate virus could be identified with a lipid envelope similar to that present in these human pathogens. Similarly, for decontamination research a surrogate that precisely matches the disinfec-

---

BOX 4-1
Challenges in Identifying Suitable Surrogates

Substantial time and effort have been expended to identify appropriate surrogate organisms for *Bacillus anthracis*. *B. globigii* (recently renamed *Bacillus subtilis var niger*) was among the first surrogates identified for this organism and facilitated research on aerosol transmission of spores. In subsequent studies, it also proved to be an acceptable surrogate for chlorine disinfection studies of spores in drinking water, although it was more resistant to chlorine than *B. anthracis*. Further studies indicated that *B. thuringiensis* more closely mimics the responses of *B. anthracis* to chlorine exposure in drinking water (Rice et al., 2005). Much research was also required to establish that *B. subtilis (globigii)* is a suitable surrogate for ultraviolet susceptibility on *B. anthracis* spores (Nicholson and Galeano, 2003).

Researchers are just beginning to understand the factors that may lead to variability in spore responses to moist heat inactivation. One of the major factors in moist heat tolerance is the core water content of spores. The core moisture content varies significantly among the different species and can be further influenced by processes used to induce sporulation (Nicholson et al., 2000). Thus most of the work on heat inactivation has been done with *B. anthracis* Ames or Stern strains rather than surrogates.

tant sensitivity of the target organism is not always needed. Decontamination studies could be conducted with surrogates known to be hardier than the select agent. However, for many emergency response operations, such as a water security breach, knowing the precise disinfection criteria needed to kill or inactivate a target organism (e.g., CT, or disinfectant concentration multiplied by the contact time) is a critical asset in public health decision making.

The project to develop and implement a framework within the EPA for evaluating the sensitivity of information and categorizing that information as classified, for official use only, or available for public release has been completed. The resulting document was not available for review by this committee, although this subject relates broadly to all aspects of the EPA water security program. The committee considered the information sharing issue to be of paramount importance, and the fact that the resulting EPA framework was not publicly available is illustrative of the problem.

Two classified reports have been developed that are related to, but not directly associated with, Section 3.2 of the Action Plan: the Threat Scenarios for Buildings and Water Systems Report and the Wastewater Baseline Threat Document (EPA, 2004b; 2005j). The first report, as described previously in this chapter, ranked the most likely contamination threats to drinking water, and the EPA subsequently refined the contaminant priorities into a prioritized short list. Additional effort to prioritize the list is not needed. For the second report, the EPA worked with the Water Environment Federation to "identify and prioritize potential physical, cyber, and contamination (e.g. biological, chemical, radiological) threats and threat scenarios for the nation's wastewater treatment and collection infrastructure, including consequence analysis of adverse effects" (EPA, 2005a). These list-generating exercises based on analyses of water security threats are potentially valuable, because they help focus both the EPA's own research efforts and broader response and recovery preparedness on the most critical and probable contaminants. However, the short list of priority contaminants has not been made available to utility managers and public health departments because of security concerns, thus substantially reducing the full value of this information. Recommendations on improving information sharing of sensitive information are presented in Chapter 5.

Development of Guidance, Protocols, and Training

The Water Contaminant Information Tool (WCIT) is a Web-accessible database on contaminants for both drinking water and wastewater that has been developed to provide guidance to the broader community of utilities and public health responders. WCIT contains information such as physical properties, toxicity, fate and transport characteristics, potential early warning indicators, suggestions for sampling and analysis, likelihood of removal by drinking water and wastewater treatment, and considerations for a utility's response to an incident. WCIT was released in November 2005. Drinking water and wastewater utilities, state drinking water and wastewater programs, drinking water and wastewater associations, and federal officials can obtain access. It currently contains information on approximately 50 contaminants. Most of the contaminants in WCIT are chemicals; population of the database with information about biologic contaminants has only recently begun. The contaminants included in this tool are intended to be those that pose a security risk, but the database includes contaminants that are commonly found in water systems. As such, the tool can be used for security issues as well as everyday problems. The contaminants identified by the EPA as the highest priorities for water security (see previous section) may or may not be included in WCIT. Although much of the information in the database is publicly available elsewhere, WCIT's real value is the compilation in a single location of contaminant information specific to water that is readily available to the water industry.

Although WCIT has been released, it has large data gaps. For example, information on the efficiency of treatment technologies is missing for a number of chemicals. The EPA utilized an expert workgroup to review the WCIT input data, but the agency will need to have a continuing mechanism to provide an ongoing review of the data, in addition to some periodic review of the data fields, to identify the need to add, revise, or delete some data as the database develops (see Chapter 6 for recommendations for future WCIT support activities). WCIT offers particular value to response and recovery applications, as well as dual-use applications, assuming that the needed data are available in the database and accurate.

Assessment

The EPA has made progress in this topical area, and many of the projects in this section of the Action Plan are nearing completion, with the exception of the surrogate project, the scope of which has expanded over time. A short list of priority contaminants has been developed, although the results of this information are classified and therefore not currently available to the water and wastewater professionals who need them. One significant accomplishment is the release of WCIT, which can be useful for responding to, recovering from, and mitigating the consequences of a terrorist attack. The database will also be useful for addressing day-to-day contamination issues for the water industry. The work on surrogates could provide guidance on the attributes of suitable surrogates as well as mechanisms to answer more easily questions about pathogenic organisms, but much more work is needed.

IMPROVING ANALYTICAL METHODOLOGIES AND MONITORING SYSTEMS FOR DRINKING WATER (ACTION PLAN SECTION 3.3)

Methods to detect water contaminants are essential for responding both to deliberate and natural contamination in water systems. Detection systems need sufficient accuracy and timeliness to accomplish the task of assessing the integrity and security of the system. The EPA's research and implementation efforts related to contaminant monitoring and analysis are described in Section 3.3 of the EPA Action Plan, with Sections 3.3.b-e focusing on research and improved detection capabilities and Sections 3.3.a and 3.3.f-g focusing on implementation:

3.3.a. A "play book" (or module) for sampling and analytical response to contaminant threats and attacks on water supplies and systems;

3.3.b. New analytical hardware and associated field and laboratory analysis methodologies for biological contaminants in water, including requirements for appropriate quality assurance/quality control (QA/QC) and sampling approaches;

3.3.c. Improved analytical hardware and associated field and laboratory analysis methodologies for chemical contaminants in water, including requirements for appropriate QA/QC and sampling approaches;

3.3.d.   Monitoring technologies for biological, chemical, and radiological contaminants and threats;

3.3.e.   Drinking water "early warning systems" and early warning systems from other sectors amenable to application in the water environment;

3.3.f.   An improved and expanded, tiered laboratory capacity and capability; and

3.3.g.   Training exercises, drills, and simulation modules for analytical methodologies and monitoring systems.

Thirty-five projects are identified in the Action Plan to address these issues (see EPA, 2004a). Although at least 18 products are planned from this work (see EPA, 2005a), only 4 products have been released as of May 2006. The response protocol (or "play book") outlined in the first subset of this section (EPA, 2003b) and some preliminary guidance documents (e.g., EPA, 2005e) have been completed, and work is progressing in the remaining areas (3.3.b-g). Work under this section includes both laboratory-based analytical capabilities (3.3.b and 3.3.c) and real-time (or near-real-time) field-based monitors and warning systems (3.3.d and 3.3.e).

New Analytical Tools

Conventional hardware and methods for detection and identification of contaminants have limitations. Standardized laboratory analytical methods for detecting many of the biological threat agents do not exist for water samples, and some existing methods need to be adapted for environmental samples that have low concentrations of target analytes and interference from background materials. Therefore, improved analytical hardware and analysis methodologies need to be developed. The EPA's efforts in developing analytical tools fall into the categories of new analytical technologies and real-time monitoring systems.

New Analytical Technologies

Several new analytical technologies are being developed based on a preliminary literature review of existing analytical methods and capabilities. One project is developing and testing an automated batch-mode radiation detector in water in collaboration with the Technical Support Working Group, although this project may not merit the high priority it has been given. A quantity of radioactive materials sufficient to produce acute radiation sickness is unlikely because of solubility limits; thus, intentional contamination of a water supply with radioactive material would create a chronic, but not acute, threat. Although it is possible that a rapid detector of radioactive contamination could reduce the extent of contamination spread (and hence exposure), it is uncertain whether the cost of developing and deploying such detectors on a wide scale could be justified by the anticipated reduction in impact. Therefore, it is difficult to justify expenditure of resources for developing an automated detection device consistent with a rapid response system when the health threat is a long-term cumulative one. A chronic radiation threat might, instead, be best addressed through routine monitoring of water samples using existing radiation detection devices. Even in dual-use applications, the concentrations of natural levels of radium and radon are unlikely to fluctuate rapidly enough to merit a continuous detection system.

Real-Time Monitoring Systems

The success of real-time monitoring systems[3] (RTMSs) will depend on continued research and development. A recent report (EPA, 2005e) acknowledges that much more research is needed on sensors to achieve the ultimate goal of "detect to protect," wherein exposure is entirely eliminated, or even "detect to warn," wherein real-time sensor response can reduce exposure. EPA (2005e) states that the "designs of early warning systems are largely theoretical or in the early stages of development," and describes the current state of the art of sensors as "detect to treat," wherein sensors provide information to facilitate treatment after exposure has occurred. In EPA (2005e), the authors express the hope that "detect to warn" will be possible with more sensor research, although numerous challenges exist for implementing RTMSs that could prevent exposure. Given that useful and practicable real-time sensors may not be a reality for many years, it seems prudent for the EPA to em-

---

[3] Previously these were called early warning systems (EWSs); however, the likelihood that they would be used in distribution systems makes the RTMS terminology more appropriate. It is unlikely that the contaminants would be detected before they would reach consumers and, therefore, the EWS would not necessarily provide prior warning (Roberson and Morley, 2005a).

phasize a more modest goal of *characterization and emergency response* for this research area in the near term.

The likelihood of implementation and the conditions for which RTMSs will be effective should be considered carefully in research on RTMSs. In Chapter 2, the problem of false positives in the implementation of contaminant detection systems is discussed in the context of positive predictive value. If highly sensitive, agent-specific detectors are implemented widely regardless of threat conditions, the number of false positives and the associated response requirements may generate frustration and excess cost and ultimately lead employees to disregard the signals. Nonspecific sensors (e.g., chlorine residual, pH, turbidity) can be used to detect perturbations in water quality that may be associated with a potential intrusion event in addition to providing valuable dual-use water quality information. Nonspecific sensors are appropriate areas for RTMS research. Nonspecific sensors should not suffer from the same extent of implementation difficulties as agent-specific sensors because the prevalence of triggering events that would merit attention is higher; therefore, the positive predictive value of non-specific sensors is improved and the percentage of false positives will be reduced (see Chapter 2). Considering the current state of technology, highly sensitive, agent-specific, real-time sensors that have no dual-use benefits should only be implemented under elevated or specific threat conditions or in highly critical venues. Agent-specific sensors, however, could also be used to provide rapid onsite analysis when an intrusion event is suspected. Therefore, the committee views research on agent-specific contaminant detection systems as a lower priority and more of a long-term research goal. The committee's view is consistent with the EPA's current near-term research approach on RTMSs.

The EPA's Water Sentinel program emphasizes dual-use applications of RTMSs, using existing, nonspecific water quality monitoring devices for detecting perturbations caused by toxic agents (EPA, 2005g; 2005h; 2005i). Within the security objective embraced by Water Sentinel, RTMSs can also include public health indicators and other types of human sensory data. Some of the technologies identified in a survey of known RTMS technologies for water systems (EPA, 2005e) have been tested in pilot scale and are now being tested in full-scale applications through Water Sentinel (EPA, 2005g).

An effective alert management system supported by rigorous data fusion algorithms is a critical need for any RTMS. Data fusion is defined as the "integration of data, recorded from a multiple sensor system, together with knowledge [from other sources]" (Esteban et al., 2005). In the context of biosurveillance, a data fusion approach has been suggested in which syndromic surveillance is combined with other information such as over-the-counter drug sales, absenteeism, etc. (Introne et al., 2005). In the context of this report, it is suggested that data fusion of sensor information, perhaps from multiple sensors, with operating and maintenance information about the system (e.g., main breaks and re-pairs), weather, and other factors may provide a better approach to inci-dent detection. However, the issues associated with RTMSs and data fusion are complex and have not been well studied in the drinking water field.

Development of Guidance, Protocols, and Training

As monitoring technologies are identified, developed, and imple-mented, guidance documents and training modules will be needed for field and laboratory personnel on analytical performance and sample handling. To date, a substantial number of projects in this section can be categorized as guidance, protocols, or training. These initiatives are di-rected at many levels, from utility personnel, to public health and emer-gency responders, to the staff of analytical laboratories.

The EPA, in collaboration with the CDC, is developing a sample pre-treatment protocol for biothreat agents using an ultrafiltration method. Pretreatment of water samples is important to collect, extract, and con-centrate low levels of target analytes from water for further processing by detection protocols. Moderate progress has been made in testing these protocols, and sample runs have been performed with bacterial spores. The protocol currently involves time-consuming manual and laboratory steps, although plans have been made to automate portions of the protocol.

The Response Protocol Toolbox (Module 4) has been formulated and completed and includes general protocols for sample acquisition, concen-tration, and analysis (EPA, 2003b). The purpose of this document is to assist in planning; it is not intended to be a "roadmap" for analytical re-sponse. Ninety percent of this toolbox has been incorporated into the National Environmental Methods Index for chemical, biological, and radiological agents (NEMI-CBR).[4] In addition, a protocol has been de-

---

[4] NEMI-CBR is an Internet database that accompanies NEMI (*http://www.nemi.gov/*) but focuses on analytes of greater interest to water security. While NEMI is open to all and

veloped for analyzing chemical unknowns, which will be critical for responding to terrorist threats; the protocol has undergone testing and validation. Analytical methods for microbials, biotoxins, and radiological contaminants are still being developed for the toolbox. The EPA has also developed a handbook on existing and emerging monitoring technologies for water (EPA, 2005d) and is working to prepare standard operating procedures for the purpose of evaluating monitoring technologies. The response protocol toolbox and NEMI-CBR should be updated on a regular basis as new information and methods become available and as more stakeholders have a chance to evaluate them and suggest modifications. The Response Protocol Toolbox is a potentially important resource, but it has not been updated since its release in December 2003. A more efficient approach to the toolbox may be a Web-based tool that enables more timely revisions and real-time access to new products, technologies, and published protocols.

The Action Plan proposed several projects to assess and manage the analytical resources in the nation's laboratories as they relate to contaminants that may be involved in an attack on water systems. Many of these activities have been folded into the Water Laboratory Alliance (WLA) in response to Homeland Security Presidential Directive 9. The objectives of the WLA are to align with existing networks, such as the CDC's Laboratory Response Network, and build the nation's laboratory response capacity for analyzing water samples from both routine surveillance and triggered response activities. On a regional level, work is under way to develop and test response plans that integrate drinking water and wastewater laboratories; public health and environmental laboratories; and utility, commercial, state, and federal laboratories. Work will then be needed to adapt the regional response plans into a consistent nationwide approach (L. Mapp, EPA, personal communication, 2007). The WLA holds promise for improving the response capacity to a water security event, but to be sustainable, the WLA will need to develop strong connections to dual-use functions.

Assessment

Some activity and progress has been made in nearly every area identified in this portion of the Action Plan, but based on the information

---

contains exclusively public consensus methods, NEMI-CBR is password protected and features many methods that have not been validated.

available to this committee, the current progress is slower than originally anticipated. The development of Module 4 in the Response Protocol Toolbox and the CBR addition to NEMI are two notable and highly visible successes. Research on new methods for chemical detection is also proceeding. Monitoring technologies are recognized as key elements in the general contaminant response strategy, as well as essential components in RTMSs. Given the difficulties in implementing contaminant-specific detector systems in a practical and feasible way, the EPA has appropriately focused its research on RTMSs on nonspecific detectors with dual-use benefits, such as pH, conductance, and chlorine residual.

CONTAINING, TREATING, DECONTAMINATING, AND DISPOSING OF CONTAMINATED WATER AND MATERIALS (ACTION PLAN SECTION 3.4)

Section 3.4 of the Action Plan—Containing, Treating, Decontaminating, and Disposing of Contaminated Water and Materials—comprises the following four major objectives:

3.4.a. Improved distribution system models that can be used to more effectively protect drinking water in the event of deliberate contaminations;

3.4.b. Improved understanding and documentation of the environmental fate of contaminants in source waters, drinking water treatment plants, and the distribution system;

3.4.c. New and more effective treatment and decontamination technologies and processes for water that has been contaminated; and

3.4.d. Improved understanding and documentation of decontamination of pipes, equipment, and other materials, and when a decontaminated system can be returned to safe use.

The EPA Action Plan identifies 30 projects to address these objectives, representing nearly 25 percent of all projects in the Action Plan. The research agenda in Section 3.4 is broad, comprising development of computer software, bench- and pilot-scale experimentation, and critical assessments of existing literature. At least 28 products are anticipated from the projects in this section of the Action Plan. As of May 2006, three documents had been released, providing preliminary guidance on common approaches for treating contaminated water based on a survey of technologies and results from focused laboratory studies (EPA, 2006a; Rice et al., 2004; 2005). Two modeling tools (TEVA, MS-EPANET) were also undergoing preliminary testing.

Advances in Knowledge

EPA work on decontamination of a distribution system in the aftermath of an attack on a water system is important for improving response and recovery capacity. The success of these projects depends heavily upon experimental work and literature review to exploit existing data. Rice et al. (2005) and an accompanying fact sheet (EPA, 2005c) describe the results of a laboratory study that examined the efficacy of typical chlorination conditions at a water treatment plant to inactivate six bacterial strains and spores of anthrax (*Bacillus anthracis*) over various contact times. The efficacy of chlorination as a decontamination technique, or whether the chlorine residual leaving the water treatment plant is adequate to counter a terrorist attack made within a distribution system, was not addressed directly in this work. Both questions are difficult to answer, particularly because of the uncertainty of competing reactions that cause loss of chlorine residual and, thus, a loss in the extent of inactivation.

The EPA has initiated laboratory work necessary to develop consumer guidance for decontamination, but additional work is needed. Rice et al. (2004) describe research with the CDC on the effectiveness of covered and uncovered boiling to inactivate various strains of anthrax. Rice et al. (2004) reported that 3-5 minutes of covered boiling will inactivate the *Bacillus anthracis* spores, but other researchers (Dunahee and Weber, 2003) have recommended thermal inactivation in sealed kitchen pressure cookers operating near autoclave temperature to avoid dispersal observed in open boiling. Additional research is needed to resolve concerns over dispersal and to investigate more readily available inactivation methods, such as microwaving (see Chapter 6).

The current state of the art for decontamination strategies for pipes within the distribution system is described in Module 6 of the Response Protocol Toolbox (EPA, 2004d), which is intended as a remediation and recovery planning guide. The effectiveness of these strategies for chemical and microbial agents used in a terrorist attack, however, is not yet known. The EPA has several excellent research pipe loops at its Test and Evaluation Center in Cincinnati, Ohio, to examine the effectiveness of decontamination strategies on various distribution system pipe materials (see Figure 4-1). This ongoing laboratory work is important, and it highlights the need for surrogates for lethal biological agents to enable large-scale experimentation (see Section 3.2, Contaminant Identification, in this chapter). Hurricane Katrina offered a real-world opportunity to test the effectiveness of various decontamination strategies (NRC, 2005; see Appendix A), although no formal EPA study was conducted to harvest lessons learned.

A National Institute of Standards and Technology project that deals specifically with decontamination of water lines and appliances in buildings is currently under way. This involves fundamental research to understand the mechanisms of microbial adhesion to surfaces in a flow field and the effectiveness of decontamination agents in removing them. The goal is to develop guidance on decontaminating piping and equipment following an intentional attack, but this information will also be used to improve mathematical models at the microscale of adsorption-desorption processes (EPA, 2005a; K. Fox, EPA, personal communication, 2005).

FIGURE 4-1 Research pipe loops at the EPA's Test and Evaluation Center that are used to examine contaminant transport behavior, decontamination strategies, and contaminant monitoring approaches.
SOURCE: Photo courtesy of Scott Minamyer, EPA.

Development of Guidance, Protocols, and Training

The first guidance document published under Section 3.4 of the Action Plan was a review of point-of-use (POU) and point-of-entry (POE) devices as means of treating contaminated drinking water (EPA, 2006a). The guidance document contained a useful compendium of information on the broad capabilities and limitations of existing POU and POE treatment devices, providing dual-use value with information about the effectiveness of these devices in removing substances routinely found in drinking water. However, it is noted correctly in the report that data are lacking on the removal capabilities of POU/POE devices with exotic microbial or chemical agents that may be used by terrorists. Candidate POU and POE devices should first be challenged with microbes and chemicals on EPA's list of threat agents; this work is now under way within the NHSRC.

An important distinction is also made in EPA (2006a) between using POU/POE devices in the "reactive" and "proactive" modes. The report notes that use of POU/POE devices in a proactive mode could be risky because the performance of such devices can deteriorate with use and, thus, their effectiveness at the time of a terrorist attack may be unknown. While this may be true of conventional interventions such as provided by membrane and adsorption separation technologies, the performance of at least one other technology—superheated water treatment—would not deteriorate with time (Butler and Weber, 2005a; 2005b). The reactive mode of implementation suffers a major drawback in that policies and mechanisms for distributing and maintaining POU and POE devices will be a major hurdle to implementation. An enormous national inventory and an efficient scheme for shipment and distribution would be needed. For these reasons, the prioritization of further research in this area should consider the low likelihood of implementation of conventional POU/POE devices following a water security event and consider alternative devices in the research stages of development.

Several other guidance documents and databases remain under development as of May 2006. For example, the Drinking Water Treatability Database will eventually be added to WCIT and will include information about the effectiveness of 30 different treatment processes on the WCIT contaminants. To populate this database, data are being collected from the scientific literature and from related EPA research. However, the paucity of existing data will necessitate additional research, including considerable new experimental work or computational estimates through structure-activity relationships. A handbook for decontaminating piping and equipment is under development, and a resource guide on the aquatic fate of biological, chemical, and radiological contaminants is also planned. Fundamental physical-chemical characteristics of each contaminant are important for modeling of contaminant fate within the distribution system (e.g., attachment to pipe walls, natural attenuation during time of travel) to improve upon response and recovery. If this information is not available in the scientific literature, considerable additional experimental or computational work (e.g., with chemical structure-activity models) will be needed.

New Analytical Tools

Two important tools are expected to come out of this research area: the Threat Ensemble Vulnerability Assessment (TEVA) modeling tool for water distribution systems and the Disposal Decision Support Tools. TEVA is a modeling tool that links network contaminant fate and transport simulations with an exposure and consequence assessment through Monte Carlo simulations of terrorist points of attack. TEVA can be used to identify the most vulnerable points in the system for contamination insertion, thereby providing useful information to guide security planning. The committee was at first concerned that TEVA was being developed for the primary purpose of siting RTMS devices based on "detect to protect" or "detect to warn" capabilities, which do not currently exist. However, EPA (2005a) emphasizes TEVA's value toward responding to and mitigating the impacts of contamination events by locating the source of contamination, estimating exposure, identifying locations for sampling, and developing decontamination strategies. In the committee's view, this is the appropriate emphasis for current modeling research.

The TEVA model requires considerable modifications to the distribution system model EPANET, including allowing for interactions among multiple species (both in the bulk water and at the pipe surface) and overlaying an exposure assessment model (EPA, 2005b). Multi-Species EPANET (MS-EPANET) software is now available as part of a beta-testing program (EPA, 2006b) and allows, for example, predictions of adsorption onto pipe surfaces, which could be important for determining the effectiveness of decontamination strategies. It is not clear whether additional experimental work will be needed to determine values of any new parameters (e.g., constants that determine adsorbability of specific substances onto pipe surfaces). Far more progress is needed on the exposure assessment model, which uses a Monte Carlo simulation of attack location within the distribution system to quantify the effect of sensor location density on exposure of water customers to a chemical or biological agent.

The EPA hopes to initiate field testing of TEVA through a partnership with a Water Utility Users Group made up of American Water Works Association member utilities. Before investing heavily in field testing, which will undoubtedly be costly, the EPA should consider inviting peer review of the preliminary software.

The TEVA model not only provides a means for utilities to improve response strategies but also provides malefactors with a tool for planning an attack on a distribution system. Unlike EPANET and MS-EPANET, which will be publicly available, the EPA is not planning to allow open access to TEVA. One possibility under consideration is to allow access to members of the Water Information Sharing and Analysis Center (WaterISAC; see Box 2-1) and other similar organizations. The EPA should consider carefully the disadvantages of restricting access to TEVA. First, enforcing this limited distribution policy may be difficult given the large number of utilities that will need access. Second, restricting access could stifle development of more user-friendly software in the commercial sector.

A partially completed, Web-based suite of Disposal Decision Support Tools became available in February 2006. It allows the user to specify a scenario (e.g., facility, type of contamination, type of remediation), and the tools provide an estimate of the mass/volume of wastes to be disposed and specify appropriate disposal facilities for each state. The present version includes a placeholder module for a "Water System Materials Disposal Decision Support Tool." The content of this section will specifically address methods for disposing of water from the remediation of contaminated buildings.

Assessment

Section 3.4 of the EPA Action Plan comprises an essential and extensive array of projects to improve response and recovery from a water security event, while also providing dual-use benefits applicable to day-to-day operations or to the response to natural disasters. The number of products completed thus far from Section 3.4 is rather modest, representing only about 20 percent of the products proposed. The initial products were understandably aimed at guidance documents and databases that could be developed readily from existing knowledge and from laboratory experiments that could be conducted quickly. Many knowledge gaps are apparent with respect to the physical-chemical characteristics of the targeted chemical and microbial agents. For this reason, users of the first generation of EPA products will likely find the guidance lacking in specificity, and more research will be needed to improve upon the guidance produced thus far. Many of the products that remain in progress rely upon laboratory experiments and development of mathematical models, and it is probable that much of this work will need to continue well beyond 2006.

PLANNING FOR CONTINGENCIES AND ADDRESSING INFRASTRUCTURE INTERDEPENDENCIES (ACTION PLAN SECTION 3.5)

The EPA's work to address contingencies and infrastructure interdependencies in this section of the Action Plan is divided into the following three subsets:

3.5.a.   Assessment of water supply alternatives;
3.5.b.   Evaluation of improved technologies and approaches for providing water in the event of both long-term and short-term disruptions; and
3.5.c.   An improved understanding of water system interdependencies with other infrastructure sectors.

According to the EPA Action Plan (EPA, 2004a), eight projects were envisioned to address these issues. Although nine products are planned from this work, no reports or products have been released as of May 2006. Work is progressing on the first and the last subsets of this section (3.5.a and 3.5.c), but little, if any, effort is being expended on the second subset, which focuses on new technologies.

New Analytical Tools

An understanding of water system interdependencies and cascading consequences from disruptions to water systems is needed because infrastructure elements can affect water systems and water systems can impact other infrastructure elements. Argonne National Laboratory (ANL) is conducting work to identify interdependencies between water and wastewater systems and other elements of the broad infrastructure (A. Hais, EPA, personal communication, 2005). As originally conceived, the objective of ANL's work was to develop a computer model called RE-STORE, patterned after ANL's Critical Infrastructures Interdependencies Integrator (CI^3) repair and recovery model developed for natural gas delivery systems. The CI^3 model is used to simulate the processes needed to repair a natural gas pipeline break and to estimate delays in restoration of gas service to assist managers in recovery planning. The EPA thought that a similar tool for water systems would help water utilities assess their vulnerabilities with respect to interdependencies, minimize outages, reduce cascading effects, and improve restoration of service. After discussions with representatives of the water industry, the EPA determined that a model that focused on water system restoration, especially pipelines, was not needed because utilities were already well positioned to assess and repair disruptions in service. The RESTORE modeling effort has now been redirected to examine the sequence of events after a contamination event. The RESTORE model would, for example, simulate a contamination event and itemize the necessary actions (e.g., sensor detection, identification of the source and cause of the sensor excursion, assessment of the extent of the contamination and potential health effects) and the time required before the utility would know enough to inform the public. Emphasis is also directed at integrating the TEVA model (see Section 3.4 in this chapter) with RESTORE to provide estimates of the health impacts from contamination events and improve the notification process. ANL has also been tasked with developing a model to estimate the overall economic impacts of a given contamination event (R. Janke, EPA, personal communication, 2006). These are reasonable project objectives that have evolved appropriately, considering stakeholder input. Additionally, these tools might be useful for preparing for or responding to natural contamination events.

Development of Guidance, Protocols, and Training

Preparation of guidance documents on water supply alternatives is an important near-term activity, considering both the need for back-up supplies in response to a terrorist incident and their dual-use value, such as in the case of natural disasters or system failures. In the aftermath of Hurricane Katrina, water supply rapidly became a critical factor, and the

U.S. Navy deployed its 100,000-gallon-per-day portable treatment unit to Mississippi. Louisiana did not accept a similar offer from the Navy apparently because Louisiana officials believed that the Navy's portable system would have to be certified and permitted as a new water system. This incident highlights the need for emergency planners to know what resources for alternative water supplies are available, on what time schedule systems can be imported, and what regulations need to be addressed in anticipation of a disaster.

The USACE is contracted to conduct studies on water supply alternatives with the objective of developing written guidance on how to secure or deploy alternative supplies following service disruption. The first three parts of the study will (1) analyze case studies for different situations, (2) assess the capabilities of existing and planned portable treatment systems, and (3) assess inherent or potential water system redundancies with the objective of identifying best practices. Much of the study is focused on ascertaining from the literature and desktop engineering evaluations what alternatives and redundancies already exist. However, a number of states and large utilities have implemented contingency plans that include interconnection of water supplies, prepositioning of bottled water, and other mutual-aid efforts, and such plans are well known to EPA and provide a basis for gathering information on best practices. This work was scheduled originally for completion in early 2005 but the results have still not been published as of January 2007.

The projects to evaluate innovative technologies for supplying both long-term and short-term drinking water supplies also seem to offer value to improving emergency response, but no apparent progress to date has been made. These activities may be more appropriate to a long-term research effort, and the findings should be added to the guidance document associated with the evaluation of existing water supply alternatives.

An additional project conducted by Lockheed Martin focuses on evaluating the application of geographic information system (GIS) technologies to water system security. Based on preliminary findings, it appears that GIS systems have broad application in water system security planning, emergency response, and remediation in addition to their importance as operational tools for utilities (N. Lewis, EPA, personal communication, 2006). For example, in a contamination event, utilities could use GIS to identify hospitals and other "critical" users for provision of available alternative water supplies. GIS has the potential to help water utilities in many other ways, such as helping to identify the source of contamination events by mapping disease outbreak, consumer complaint locations, and the spread of contamination. GIS could also link distribution system information to "reverse 911" systems to notify water users quickly and directly in the case of a natural or deliberate contamination event. From these preliminary findings, additional technical support efforts to facilitate better integration of GIS applications into crisis management planning are warranted (see Chapter 6 for future research recommendations).

In the National Research Council's review of the EPA Action Plan (NRC, 2004) it was suggested that "failure of the human subsystem" is an area of research not covered by the research agenda. In other words, water and wastewater systems may well be compromised by incapacitation of plant operators, either through major natural outbreaks or bioterrorism attacks that result in widespread illness. Such planning has substantial dual-use value, and this research deserves more attention (see Chapter 6).

Assessment

Overall, it appears that the work in Section 3.5, Planning for Contingencies and Addressing Infrastructure Interdependencies, has not received high priority in EPA's research program, and as a result, the products are behind schedule or in some cases projects have not been started. The research now being performed by USACE, Lockheed Martin, and ANL addresses important topics for emergency preparedness and response for disaster events, and the guidance products from this work might have been of great value for response and recovery efforts following Hurricane Katrina had they been available sooner.

TARGETING IMPACTS ON HUMAN HEALTH AND INFORMING THE PUBLIC ABOUT RISKS (ACTION PLAN SECTION 3.6)

Priority items for the EPA to accomplish in the area of risk assessment and risk communication are identified in Section 3.6 of the Action Plan, which is divided into five areas:

3.6.a. An improved understanding of multiple routes of exposure of contaminants in drinking water supplies and systems;

3.6.b.   Improved communication in health surveillance to rapidly identify and control a disease outbreak associated with contaminated drinking water;

3.6.c.   Evaluation of the usefulness and validity of nontraditional data sources for the derivation of acute and chronic toxicity values applied to water;

3.6.d.   Risk assessment/risk management framework for identifying the impact of containment, decontamination, treatment, and disposal options and the subsequent response; and

3.6.e.   Methods and means to communicate risks to local communities and to respond to customers in case of an attack on drinking water systems.

Fifteen projects were identified in EPA (2004a) to address these issues, although progress on these projects appears slow (see NRC, 2004). Work is under way in all of the subsets of this section, and at least 12 products are planned from this work (see EPA, 2005a). As of May 2006, no products had been released publicly, although a few risk assessment tools have been released in limited distribution for testing purposes, and several workshops had been conducted.

Advances in Knowledge

The EPA contracted with Battelle to conduct a study on the generation of bioaerosols during showering, and further studies on direct and indirect exposure pathways have been initiated. Exposure and dose-response studies may provide new information useful to mitigate health impacts after a terrorist attack and are appropriate high-priority projects that have practical dual-use applications. For example, if the risk of illness from showering or toilet flushing using contaminated water is shown to be high, emergency response guidance at the local and federal level recommending "no use" water advisories could be developed and implemented. If the risk is shown by this research to be very low, "no use" water advisories could be discouraged and replaced with specific public health messages that would be helpful in further reducing the risk to water users.

A preliminary risk assessment framework and methodology for assessing risks from exposure to biological agents in water systems is being developed with Syracuse Research Corporation. A microbial risk framework has substantial benefits beyond application to terrorist threats and parallels already mature frameworks (EPA, 1998; 2005l) for assessing risk from chemicals (e.g., carcinogens, neurotoxins). Risk assessments are of high priority to any response and recovery effort. The risk assessment framework project, however, appears to be more than a year behind schedule, and it is not clear that the risk assessment/risk management projects are being integrated into the other phases of water security research rather than being isolated.

Two major ongoing efforts are being supported to fuse health effects data (syndromic surveillance) and environmental information into early warning systems: Real-time Outbreak and Disease Surveillance (RODS) and Electronic Surveillance System for the Early Notification of Community-Based Epidemics (ESSENCE). RODS, which is being developed by the University of Pittsburgh, is being piloted in the city of Pittsburgh, and information on water quality is being integrated to ascertain the utility of such real-time information. ESSENCE, developed by Johns Hopkins University (Lombardo et al., 2004), is also being pilot-tested. These methods hold promise for early detection of health impacts, serve a dual-use purpose for the detection of naturally occurring waterborne contamination events, and are potentially useful in water terrorism events (Ashford et al., 2003; Meinhardt, 2005). The EPA is part of a steering committee (with the CDC) developing and beta-testing the RODS and ESSENCE systems. The EPA is hoping to pilot-test the systems until 2009. The RODS and ESSENCE surveillance research will also examine practical risk communication protocols that might be implemented when, based on surveillance data, it appears that the public's health may be at risk from a water contamination event. The EPA has been working with Washington, DC, Cincinnati, and other municipal utilities at integrating various data streams on health and water into an integrated monitoring program (C. Sonich-Mullin, EPA, communication, 2006). Nonfederal parties (e.g., state agencies, academic or professional societies like the International Disease Surveillance Society) should also be brought into these discussions.

None of the additional research projects proposed in NRC (2004) to advance the knowledge on communication of risks to the public have been initiated. Also, no new studies have been initiated related to a formal analysis of the risks and benefits of releasing or withholding of information due to security concerns. These recommended research projects are discussed further in Chapter 6.

Development of Guidance, Protocols, and Training

The EPA participated in weapons of mass destruction exercises and cosponsored tabletop exercises with the Department of Energy, the Office of Counterterrorism, and the U.S. Coast Guard. These exercises have been helpful in bringing together the water and energy communities, facilitating discussion about back-up power generation and enabling the water community to educate the energy community about what priorities are important in an emergency situation (Kathy Clayton and C. Sonich-Mullin, EPA, personal communication, 2005). Continued effort in this area is necessary—perhaps through the Office of Water—as agencies that are likely to be involved in a water security incident do not typically have experience in establishing and maintaining these types of collaborative relationships.

The EPA has contracted the services of the Center for Risk Communication to develop a risk communication guidebook for likely scenarios, provide training, and conduct message mapping workshops. Message mapping is a tool "for achieving message clarity and conciseness" that serves as a "visual aid and roadmap for displaying detailed, hierarchically organized responses to anticipated high concern issues, questions, or concerns."[5] All of these activities are under way but have yet to be completed. Entities that have received training include water utilities, public health department surveillance and information officers, homeland security managers, public information officers, emergency responders, and on-scene coordinators. The message mapping workshops have not been subjected to actual situations in which water quality is compromised, so the usefulness of this particular communication tool in real-life water security situations is unknown. However, the tool has been used in other homeland security incidents, including the attack on the World Trade Center and the London subway bombings (K. Fox, EPA, personal communication, 2007).

Improved risk communication has significant dual-purpose value, as these skills would also be needed in the case of a natural contamination event or a natural disaster. The EPA is developing risk communication templates for various terrorism scenarios to assist jurisdictions in their communication planning. In May 2004, the Office of Water and the NHSRC cosponsored the National Water Security Risk Communication Symposium (EPA, 2005k). This symposium served as an information exchange among various stakeholders, and recommendations coming out

---

[5] *http://www.centerforriskcommunication.org/services.htm.*

of this symposium may be useful in the development of a national training program.

Data dictionaries have been developed to allow risk assessors to obtain relevant information about contaminants quickly, without having to resort to evaluating chemicals using a weight-of-evidence approach. The data dictionaries are now available to risk assessors on a secure site and will eventually be expanded for public access.

No plans are in place to conduct a formal evaluation of these efforts to test the effectiveness in reaching key audiences.

New Analytical Tools

The EPA has developed a scenario-driven tool, the Consequence Assessment Tool (CAT), designed to work together with WCIT to evaluate risk in a contamination event. The tool allows the user to determine exposure point concentrations and assess risk, based on information on the population, pathway, receptors, exposure rate, and duration. The CAT/WCIT programs can also provide toxicity data, and with time, the EPA hopes to attach confidence intervals to the data presented. The CAT provides risk management options, treatment options, cleanup levels, and links to necessary personal protective gear. The actual utility of such tools needs to be tested directly with potential users, including first responders.

The CAT/WCIT tools have gaps with respect to toxicity data for certain chemicals for which low-dose information is not available. In the Action Plan, the use of Quantitative Structure Activity Relationship (QSAR) and lethal dose, 50 percent (LD_{50}; i.e., acute toxicity) information was indicated as one route to filling such gaps rapidly. The EPA is just starting the process of trying to adapt the databases of its National Center for Environmental Assessment on QSAR and LD_{50} to CAT/WCIT (K. Clayton, EPA, personal communication, 2005).

NRC (2004) noted the open-ended and ambitious nature of some of the information gathering efforts, and, as predicted, the efforts are taking longer than envisioned. NRC (2004) therefore recommended that information gathering proceed in a manner that provides useful but perhaps approximate information initially, with the gaps filled in via successive revisits. Information databases are always in danger of "the perfect becoming the enemy of the good." It is not clear whether EPA has adopted this approach or how the EPA is devoting resources to filling these information gaps, considering the size of the task and the potential time required to fill those gaps with experimental data, or how data gathering efforts are being prioritized.

Assessment

The EPA's work in risk assessment, risk management, and risk communication addresses important issues critical to response and recovery after a terrorist attack, and many of these issues have dual-use applications to natural water contamination concerns, including the aftermath of natural disasters. However, progress in this area has been slow, and few if any products have been publicly released. Although progress has been made on several risk communication projects, too little emphasis in the Action Plan has been devoted to investigating and utilizing interdisciplinary behavioral science research to better prepare various stakeholders for water security incidents. For example, what are the public's beliefs, opinions, and knowledge about water security risks, how do risk perception and other psychological factors affect individual or family responses to water-related events and disease prevention messages, and how can the EPA, water and wastewater professionals, and public health officials effectively communicate these risks with the public? Suggestions for additional research needs are discussed further in Chapter 6.

WASTEWATER TREATMENT AND COLLECTION SYSTEM PROJECTS (ACTION PLAN SECTION 4.0)

Work on wastewater systems is now currently under way, both by the EPA alone and with a variety of partners. The principal areas of investigation identified by the EPA are as follows:

4.0.a. Identification of threats;

4.0.b. Assessment of the potential health and safety risks resulting from contaminated wastewater facilities;

4.0.c. Improved intrusion monitoring and surveillance technologies;

4.0.d. Improved designs for wastewater systems to reduce vulnerability to physical threats;

4.0.e. Enhanced prevention and response planning methods; and

4.0.f.   Methods and means to securely maintain and, when appropriate, transmit information on contaminants, and threat scenarios applicable to wastewater systems.

Twenty-two projects are identified in the Action Plan to address these issues. Work is being conducted in all of the above subsets, and as of May 2006 three products had been produced focused on the identification of threats to wastewater systems (EPA, 2005j), the development of interim design standards (ASCE et al., 2004b), and planning guidance for utilities for handling decontamination wastewater (NACWA, 2005). Most of the effort in this area involves data gathering, analysis, and synthesis, rather than collecting new data or developing new analytical tools or technologies. At least six additional products were anticipated from this work (EPA, 2005a).

Advances in Knowledge

The EPA is working to identify and prioritize potential physical, cyber, and contamination threats and threat scenarios for the nation's wastewater treatment and collection infrastructure, including consequence analysis, and has prepared a classified baseline threat document for wastewater systems (EPA, 2005j). The EPA is also planning projects to assess the current practices and methods to control intrusion into wastewater collection systems and other components of the wastewater infrastructure (including combined systems and stormwater systems) that could be used as conduits for explosive attacks on critical community targets. Work is under way with Argonne National Laboratory to assess the impacts on wastewater and drinking water from a community attack from a radiological dispersal device (A. Hais, EPA, personal communication, 2005). The data that are to be gathered are not considered groundbreaking, but the work is needed to understand more fully the nature and magnitude of the threat.

Development of Guidance, Protocols, and Training

A critical element in implementing new analytical tools and research findings in the wastewater sector will be the availability of accessible, readable, and easily comprehensible guidance, protocols, and training materials and their dissemination. As in the drinking water projects, the

EPA plans to develop a response protocol toolbox to help wastewater utilities create their own plans for responding to threats or attacks. Other guidance documents in development that may help improve response and recovery efforts include a guide to managing contamination events for wastewater, guidance on detection systems, and information on the efficacy of treatment methods for a variety of contaminants. The EPA plans to analyze potential alternatives to chlorine disinfection for wastewater because accidental or intentional releases of large quantities of chlorine gas pose serious public health and safety concerns. The National Association of Clean Water Agencies (NACWA, 2005) developed useful guidance for utilities on handling decontamination wastewater. Interim voluntary design standards for wastewater utilities have been developed (ASCE et al., 2004b) that offer guidance for new construction, reconstruction, and retrofitting for wastewater systems, with a focus on security in combination with improved operations. Consistent with the recommendation in NRC (2004), this approach recognizes the importance of dual use to the successful implementation of security measures.

New Analytical Tools

The EPA is working with WERF to develop a software model known as SewerNet. The software is currently under development as a tool to assess and improve emergency preparedness. The GIS-based software should allow wastewater utilities to assess the effect of a variety of malicious events, including the release of biological or chemical agents into the wastewater collection system.

Much of the work being undertaken in the water sector with respect to sensor development may have applications in the wastewater sector with further development specific to the challenges of the wastewater setting. The Action Plan includes a project to test and evaluate existing monitoring and surveillance technologies in wastewater systems.

Assessment

The projects identified for the wastewater sector are rational, reasonable first steps that reflect the major concerns with respect to the security issues confronting the wastewater collection and treatment infrastructure.

Some useful guidance has been developed, but the delivery of products has been slow. The proposed and ongoing EPA projects are important steps in helping to organize the disparate information that now exists related to wastewater security. As the various investigations proceed, data gaps and technology needs will likely be identified. However, how these research needs will be addressed and what strategy will be used to assign priorities to the various tasks is not clear.

IMPLEMENTATION (ACTION PLAN SECTION 5.0)

Section 5.0 of the Action Plan incorporates several initiatives that relate to implementation of the Action Plan. Two of these initiatives—the Technology Testing and Evaluation Program and Information Sharing—are reviewed below.

Technology Testing

The Technology Testing and Evaluation Program (TTEP) seeks to advance effective security-related technologies by rigorously testing their performance and making this information available to end users. To date, the TTEP program has tested such technologies as portable cyanide analyzers, rapid toxicity testing systems, reverse osmosis POU devices, and multiparameter water quality probes. TTEP is a positive outgrowth of the EPA's Environmental Technology Verification (ETV) program, which focused entirely on commercially ready technologies, required vendor participation and partial vendor funding, and involved negotiations with vendors over how test results would be reported. However, TTEP improved the program by including testing of both commercially available technologies and technologies in various stages of research and development and not requiring vendors to pay a fee for testing. Now, the EPA can select and evaluate any commercially available technology (with or without vendor permission) and use test protocols designed to address specific security applications rather than those deemed satisfactory to the vendor. Another important objective of TTEP is to provide test data and reports that are useful to end users. Specifically, TTEP provides side-by-side performance product comparisons that enable users to evaluate their security product alternatives more easily. Lastly, the working relationship between the contractor who performs the tests (Battelle) and the EPA has been changed from a cooperative agreement under

ETV to a contractual relationship under TTEP. This legal relationship allows the EPA better access to specific Battelle infrastructure and personnel, more influence over which types of test protocols will be developed, and involvement in determining how specific technologies will be evaluated.

While TTEP seems to be an improved mechanism for testing technologies that are touted as homeland security solutions or those that look promising to stakeholders or other government agencies, it introduces new challenges. First the scope of the agents of interest is broad (e.g., pathogenic bacteria, parasites, and viruses; bacterial toxins; chemical warfare agents; toxic industrial chemicals; radionuclides). The EPA will need to identify which technologies exist or are in development for this broad array of agents and intervention methods, identify which technologies have substantial potential for water security applications (as well as dual-use applications), and then decide how to prioritize testing for the most promising technologies under TTEP. Developing suitable test protocols is also a challenge. Test protocols may differ considerably depending on the technology being evaluated and the threat agent. Battelle's capacity to rapidly develop new test protocols and to evaluate different types of equipment in any single year is unclear. Regardless, the EPA has limits on the funds available to support the TTEP program, which is just one component of its long-term water security research and technical support agenda. Recommendations for prioritizing TTEP's efforts are provided in Chapter 6.

Communication of Research Findings

Although the EPA is in its fourth year of the Action Plan, the number of products released to date is limited. Of the more than 75 products anticipated to result from the Action Plan (not including testing reports from the TTEP program), as of September 2005, only 11 products had been released, and of these, 3 are either classified or restricted access (EPA, 2005a). As of May 2006, an additional five products had been publicly released, although several tools had been released in limited distribution for testing purposes. Assessing the success of the entire program based on a limited number of products is difficult and may not be representative.

Information sharing is one of the most critical issues facing the EPA's water security research program. EPA staff insist that the vast majority of the findings from the research program will be widely available to anyone (K. Nickel, EPA, personal communication, 2005), but the committee has some concerns that critical information may not be reaching those who need it. For example, the list of priority contaminants is important for utilities that may want to establish their own security-focused sampling program or simply improve their emergency response capacity, but this information has been classified and cannot be shared with utilities, even over secure dissemination mechanisms.

Many of the findings are only valuable if they can be distributed in a manner that allows stakeholders to easily locate the material, recognize its value, and comprehend the relevant information. The publicly available research products are posted at the EPA's Water Infrastructure Protection Web page,[6] and fact sheets are also provided to summarize each of the products available. The EPA has also reached out to utility stakeholders through its Water Sector Security Workshops to publicize ongoing research efforts and solicit informal feedback from utilities. The vast number of anticipated reports, tools, and databases, however, will undoubtedly make it difficult for utilities to keep up with new information. To help address this concern, the NHSRC is utilizing Rich Site Summary (RSS) technology and e-mail subscriber lists to push notices of new material to registered users. These efforts are to be commended, but more work could improve the navigability of the EPA water security Web sites for a broader community of stakeholders. Currently, research products are spread across multiple NHSRC Web pages organized by subject area, and the presence of two separate EPA water security Web sites (Office of Water[7] and the NHSRC) that are not clearly linked is likely to further confuse interested stakeholders. Specific recommendations for improving the information sharing strategies, including methods for disseminating sensitive materials, are discussed in Chapter 5.

Among the research products produced from the program to date, the committee found a few useful products and tools that seem appropriately targeted to end users (e.g., WCIT, AT Planner; NACWA, 2005). The EPA initiated pilot-testing programs for several of its tools and databases with representative stakeholders to improve the usefulness of these products. However, the EPA should take full advantage of research opportunities to further improve the dissemination and the effectiveness of the research products (see Chapter 5). Other early documents represent exhaustive synopses of existing material that will provide important foundations for future research, but contain too many information gaps to

---

[6] *http://www.epa.gov/nhsrc/wip.htm.*
[7] *http://www.epa.gov/safewater/security/.*

provide direct and practical homeland security guidance to utilities (e.g., EPA, 2005e; 2006a). Some products, such as the Response Protocol Toolbox, require extensive training to be used appropriately. Other research products were not available to the general public because of security constraints (e.g., EPA, 2004b; 2005j).

A principal task that remains is to prepare a meaningful synthesis of the information and data developed from the completed and ongoing research projects. The synthesis step is of critical importance if the information and data developed in the water and wastewater security research program are to be of use to individual utilities and municipal agencies.

SUMMARY AND CONCLUSIONS

Important progress has been made in implementing the EPA's water security research and technical support program described in the Action Plan, but many of the projects have been delayed behind the originally anticipated timelines (see NRC, 2004; Appendix A), and relatively few products had been publicly released during the committee's review. The reasons for the delays were varied, and many were specific to the individual circumstances of the subject matter, personnel, or contractors involved. The Action Plan was ambitious in scope and its original timelines may have been overly optimistic. With the passage of time since the last major terrorist attack on the United States, the pressure for fast results also seems to have faded, even though the anticipated Action Plan products, with careful management, could yield results useful for improving the nation's water security and its response and recovery capacity. Overall, the EPA water security program has initiated research and technical projects that address important issues and seek to address critical gaps in knowledge. Many of the EPA projects under way could also have valuable dual-use benefits.

Tools have been developed and information generated in several key areas. Priority contaminants have been identified, and this process has served as a means to prioritize the EPA's other research efforts. Numerous tools have been developed, including WCIT, MS-EPANET, AT Planner, and the CAT, that will help users improve terrorism preparedness and response capabilities. Protocols for contaminant analysis have been identified or developed, and analytical methods for priority water security contaminants have been incorporated in the NEMI-CBR database. Research is also under way to test the application of current RTMS technologies, appropriately emphasizing nonspecific detection devices with dual-use applications. Risk communication strategies have been developed and communication workshops held to improve response strategies in case of a water security event. Basic laboratory research is also under way to identify surrogates and to fill critical gaps in the current understanding of the fate and transport and exposure risks for water security agents. Among the EPA's implementation activities, modifications have been made to the TTEP that should improve both the effectiveness of the process and the value of the results to end users.

Other areas, such as physical and cyber security, contingency planning, and wastewater security, have shown weaker or somewhat disjointed progress due to the relative low priority of these areas to the EPA. Also, the EPA's lack of expertise in these areas has meant that much of the work has taken place outside the EPA, and contract management alone affords limited oversight and guidance to the work being performed. Identifying and assessing the relative importance of physical and cyber threats remains a gap that has critical implications on the prioritization of efforts within the water security research program. Gaps also exist in developing visionary designs for water and wastewater systems and incorporating behavioral science research to better prepare stakeholders for water security incidents. These issues are addressed in more detail in Chapters 5 and 6.

An important issue that remains unresolved is making water security information accessible to those who might need it. The results of the water security program will only be valuable if they are distributed in a manner that allows stakeholders to easily locate the material, recognize its value, and understand the relevant findings. The problem of information sharing in a security context is one of the most difficult the EPA faces. Currently, some important information on contaminants and threats that could improve utilities response capabilities is being withheld due to security concerns.

5

Recommendations for Improving
Program Implementation

The Environmental Protection Agency's (EPA's) water security research program originated in 2002 under pressure to enhance scientific information and technical support related to homeland security, despite many gaps in our understanding and little if any synthesis of existing knowledge. The EPA rapidly developed a research infrastructure and the Water Security Research and Technical Support Action Plan (EPA, 2004a) to address these short-term information needs using a three- to four-year time horizon. When it became clear that the information needs could not be addressed fully in the short term, the EPA's National Homeland Security Research Center (NHSRC) was made permanent, and the Water Infrastructure Protection Division was formed.

With the passage of time, the EPA has now had a chance to gain some perspective on which projects deserve more emphasis and which less, which projects have been understaffed or underfunded with respect to their importance in the larger picture, and which projects are simply inappropriate for the agency in its current circumstances and capabilities. The NHSRC is now at a transition point, when it can put this perspective into a useable form as the EPA plans its next steps for the Water Infrastructure Protection Division. In this chapter, program implementation issues are analyzed, looking ahead to a vision of the EPA's water security research program and to the past to identify lessons learned from the experiences of the first four years. Specifically, the committee presents recommendations for strategic planning, research management, and information sharing. These program management suggestions are meant to strengthen the EPA's water security research program further and use its limited resources to support the needs of the water and wastewater industries, public health workers, emergency responders, and citizens.

DEVELOPING A NEW STRATEGIC APPROACH FOR WATER SECURITY RESEARCH

The EPA has provided important leadership and initiative in the area of water security research, but if the agency is to sustain this leadership role, it needs to solidify and enhance a vision for its water security research program with distinct missions and objectives beyond the short-term objectives of the Action Plan (EPA, 2004a). The committee, therefore, recommends that the EPA's Water Infrastructure Protection Division formally articulate its mission and program objectives as it makes the transition beyond the Action Plan. Several suggestions are presented in this chapter to guide the EPA in developing a new strategic approach for water security research.

Strategic Program Objectives for the Future of EPA Water Security Research

The goal of the EPA's water security research program should be to create useful research products based on the best scientific knowledge at its disposal. The success of the research products can be judged by the criteria presented in Chapter 3 and reiterated here:

1. Water security threats with the greatest likelihood and potential consequences (including fatalities, sickness, economic losses, and loss of public confidence) are addressed.
2. Effectiveness and efficiency of the nation's response and recovery capacity are improved and/or risk reduction or consequence mitigation measures are developed.
3. Implementation of new technologies/methodologies is judged to be likely, taking into account their cost, usefulness, and maintenance requirements.
4. Dual-use benefits accrue from the research.

After studying the organization of the EPA's current water security research program, the committee suggests three broad program objectives to organize future water security research. These objectives were developed out of criterion 2 above and support the overarching goal of creating useful research products:

- **Develop research products to support more resilient design and operation of facilities and systems.** This objective encompasses research on pre-incident preparedness and mitigation activities, including risk and threat assessments, and is consistent with the EPA's historic emphasis on prevention of adverse effects. It also recognizes the futility of preventing an attack and focuses research on products and innovative approaches that could mitigate the impacts from an attack or improve the resiliency of systems to recover. Work supporting this objective will likely have multiple benefits since resilient designs and operations should also speed recovery from natural disasters or nonintentional system failures. If the EPA embraces this objective, the agency will need to communicate its vision of resilient systems and help broaden the perceptions of security beyond fences and alarms.

- **Better enable operators and responders to detect and assess incidents.** This objective encompasses research on contamination detection and analysis methods and distribution system modeling tools to assess the probable spread of contamination. Research in support of this objective will help minimize consequences from water security incidents and shorten the time before response and recovery actions can be taken. The focus on detection and assessment parallels other EPA programs, such as those focusing on incident assessment (e.g., under the Comprehensive Environmental Response, Compensation, and Liability Act [CERCLA]).

- **Improve response and recovery.** This objective emphasizes research that enhances post-incident activities, which aligns with the historic work of the EPA on mitigation and cleanup. Contingency planning, risk assessment, risk communication, and decontamination are all included in this research objective.

These three program objectives are offered as one way to organize the future water security research priorities, emphasizing pre-incident, incident, and post-incident applications. These proposed objectives are consistent with the criteria outlined in Chapter 3, although other organizing frameworks are certainly feasible.

Strategic Research Planning and Prioritization

Once the program objectives are identified, strategic research planning is needed to identify and organize the tasks necessary to achieve the objectives. An updated analysis of the state of the science and water security risks (considering probable physical, cyber, and contaminant threats) is needed for the EPA to identify those risks deserving at least some research attention. Although the Department of Homeland Security (DHS) has criteria for determining its research priorities (e.g., focusing on threat scenarios for which the number of casualties is predicted to be greater than 10,000), the EPA should use this opportunity to articulate its own criteria for defining research needs considering other important issues such as loss of public confidence or applications to natural disasters.

The four criteria presented in Chapter 3 can be used to prioritize future water security research projects within the core program objectives. Additionally, the EPA can and should address the following questions in setting its research priorities:

• What key gaps exist in the current state of water security science and technology that should be addressed in the near term to meet the particular program objectives?
• What are the trade-offs with respect to cost, potential benefit, and degree of urgency?

Utility managers and other end users of the research products can provide valuable insight on these questions and should be included in the strategic planning process.

Once research projects have been identified and prioritized to address the overarching program objectives, the EPA should identify appropriate research partners and other research entities that can help conduct this research. The EPA's research vision for water security should not be limited to those topics within its traditional expertise or even those subjects that can be reasonably funded within the EPA's research budget. By maintaining a broad vision for water security research, the EPA can engage other entities (e.g., the National Science Foundation, DHS, private industry) to join in the efforts to accomplish the research objectives.

A strategic planning exercise is a logical and necessary extension of the Action Plan. Although it is beyond the committee's charge to recommend a specific strategic planning model, the EPA will need to investigate existing planning and decision-making models before embarking on this endeavor to ensure a successful and appropriately inclusive planning process. A new strategic approach to water security research should strengthen the EPA's leadership in the field while emphasizing valuable research products that can guide the most important aspects of pre-incident, incident, and post-incident water security activities.

RESEARCH MANAGEMENT

The water security research program presents challenging management issues, as noted in Chapter 2. Suggestions are provided below with respect to the distribution of intramural and extramural research, strengthening the research program, and improving the mechanisms available for independent peer review.

Distribution of Intramural and Extramural Research

Much of the water security research and technical support work conducted under the Action Plan is being done by organizations outside the EPA, including other governmental organizations and nongovernmental entities. Using external contractors for a significant portion of the research portfolio was an appropriate strategy when the NHSRC was expected to have a limited lifespan and needed to address a great number of research questions in a short time. Now that the NHSRC has been made permanent, the pros and cons of using contracts as the principal management tool for conducting research in areas the EPA is not currently staffed or equipped to handle should be reassessed. Should the NHSRC continue to maintain competence only in the EPA's traditional strength areas, such as contaminant occurrence, fate and effects, treatment and conveyance, and agent detection? Or should the NHSRC broaden its base of skills to address a wider array of security threats (e.g., cyber security, blasts) and research topics (e.g., behavioral science, information management)?

The major *disadvantages* of contracting a large portion of the water security research portfolio include the following:

- Contracting does not strengthen internal NHSRC capability, allowing some important gaps in NHSRC expertise to persist over long time frames. If the EPA were to build its staff knowledge and skills by conducting more research in-house, these skills could also provide a long-term asset to the EPA, because this knowledge could be applied to other research problems and could enhance the information resources immediately available during emergency events and natural disasters.

• Excessive dependence on contracting may hinder the development of the precise skills and knowledge required for EPA staff to prepare and manage external research contracts effectively. Adequate contract oversight necessitates that one or more persons at the NHSRC be capable of writing an effective scope of work, monitoring the progress of the contract, and interpreting the results in the context of a water security application. This usually entails identifying, in advance, research obstacles and other technical problems that may arise. Successfully accomplishing the NHSRC goals through a contract is unlikely if the NHSRC has no research staff with the appropriate expertise to manage the contract. The research skills that are needed to prepare and monitor the progress of contracts are likely to erode with time as individuals become engaged as full-time project officers rather than continuing to conduct research themselves.

• Contracting limits the EPA's understanding of the strengths and weaknesses of the research and reduces opportunities for addressing problems or concerns during the course of the project. Offsite research usually does not allow for frequent face-to-face meetings and direct review of laboratory work. When research is conducted in-house, problems can be identified and protocols modified immediately without lengthy delays, negotiations, or cost overruns.

• Contracting mechanisms limit the degree of flexibility in setting or changing research priorities in response to new information, emergencies, or shifting agency priorities.

There are also clear *advantages* of contracting to complement the expertise of EPA staff and to select the best and most knowledgeable researchers to conduct advanced research projects. In the following specific circumstances, contracting may offer notable advantages to the EPA:

• When the EPA lacks major equipment or specialized facilities that may be needed only for a limited number of experiments.

• When NHSRC staff lack skills, and researchers at another facility are highly skilled in the type of research and equipment required. Even in this situation, however, the NHSRC needs to have a project officer with sufficient subject matter expertise to develop and monitor the contract and interpret and integrate the results.

• When beneficial collaborative relationships between the NHSRC and non-NHSRC researchers could result from the contract.

- When fast results are required and well-established protocols exist. Contractors can supply additional personnel to carry out required tasks, perhaps using NHSRC equipment and facilities, to supplement EPA staffing capabilities. Thus, contracting can be used to achieve staffing flexibility.

- When two or more new methods with slightly different analytical approaches need to be developed and evaluated for comparison purposes. Components of a large study can be completed by multiple contractors, and the best method can be either adopted by the NHSRC or used as the starting point for further development by NHSRC researchers.

- When the contractor is located in close proximity to a field study site and can facilitate the collection and/or analysis of environmental samples.

In summary, advantages and disadvantages exist to using contracts and other external funding mechanisms for conducting water security research. Based on the advantages, extramural funding should be used to support specific research in the EPA water security research program. Careful attention, however, should be given to achieving the right balance. The EPA should develop greater in-house research capability, or at least subject matter expertise, in disciplines that have been historically weak and where long-term water security concerns are projected. Such areas include physical security and behavioral sciences (see Chapter 4).

The NHSRC should make a conscious decision about the necessary balance of skills among its personnel and rebalance its permanent staff lines in accordance with that decision. As noted above, even if research is to be conducted via contracts, the EPA needs adequate in-house expertise to evaluate and manage such contracts. Many other EPA programs have evolved in a similar manner. For example, the startup of the EPA hazardous waste program occurred via the transfer of individuals from solid waste, water, and other programs. As the permanence of the endeavor became clear, the skill set of permanent staff changed to address the technical needs of the program (e.g., by adding individuals with focused skills in earth sciences and chemical and geotechnical engineering).

Strengthening the EPA Research Program

The administrative and technical staff in the laboratories, centers, and offices of the EPA's Office of Research and Development (ORD) are critical resources to support innovative research and work in partnership with extramural researchers to achieve the NHSRC's goals. However, a high percentage of the EPA's current scientists and engineers will soon reach retirement age. Planning is under way to address this issue within the ORD's Management Multi-Year Plan (EPA, 2005f). Three comprehensive management initiatives, designated strategic goals, are slated to be completed within the next three years, and one of the goals is to attract, develop, and retain a talented and diverse workforce. Activities which support this goal include (1) creating the next generation of scientists through efforts such as the STAR Fellowship Program, the AAAS Environmental and Risk Policy Fellows Programs, the Association of Schools of Public Health Fellows Program, the ORD postdoctoral employee program, support for minority academic institutions, and support for state and national science fairs; and (2) implementing initiatives to strengthen the ORD in attracting and retaining a well-qualified workforce, as outlined in EPA (2004e). These initiatives are an important step that should be supported by the NHSRC leadership.

The EPA could also employ a number of possible underutilized mechanisms to enhance its onsite expertise without adding permanent staffing. For example, the National Science Foundation relies upon the use of "rotators" hired under the Intergovernmental Personnel Act to manage particular research programs (or portions of programs). The use of such personnel, serving term appointments (perhaps two or three years) "on loan" from the academic or private sector or from other governmental agencies, would bring a more robust set of onsite skills. This approach could also foster cross-training with EPA staff and provide further long-term benefits.

One key part of strengthening the EPA water security research program involves building alliances with relevant experts. The EPA is currently working to expand its network of experts while also improving coordination among federal agencies and nongovernment organizations through the Distribution System Research Consortium.[1] The EPA has held several meetings, including its Water Sector Security Workshops

---

[1] The Distribution System Research Consortium is an umbrella organization made up of 14 partnering federal and nonfederal organizations to advance science, technology, and research to protect water distribution systems from terrorist attack.

(EPA, 2006c), to receive input from and foster alliances with water utilities, trade organizations, local and state governments, public health organizations, and emergency responders. The EPA should also work to foster alliances with professional engineering and technical societies and to build new alliances with experts in other related fields, such as earthquake impact mitigation, disaster response, or social science related to terrorism. Continually improving collaboration with outside experts will keep the EPA abreast of new developments in the field and minimize duplication of effort.

Peer Review

Effective independent peer review is an important mechanism for avoiding research errors, program problems, and inefficiencies. Peer review applies to both project-level evaluations (including reviews of proposals and final products) and program-level reviews. The EPA has long used peer review for evaluating research proposals in its competitive grants program. The EPA has used the Science Advisory Board (SAB) to provide broad-level programmatic review, and the Homeland Security Advisory Committee was formed through the SAB in 2005 to provide focused advice to the NHSRC on homeland security issues. The ORD has also used the Board of Scientific Counselors to provide programmatic review of the agency's research programs.

Assuring appropriate independent peer review in the EPA's water security program presents particular challenges. A major challenge is providing independent peer review of NHSRC activities that contain classified, or sensitive but unclassified, material. Currently, sensitive and classified peer-review mechanisms may not be sufficient.

Sensitive and classified peer-review activities, while new to the EPA, are not new to the federal government. The EPA should examine available mechanisms to provide effective independent peer review of sensitive or classified work. The NHSRC should carefully review areas where independent peer review involving sensitive and classified material is helpful or necessary and explore some of the following options:

- The EPA could work with other governmental agencies (e.g., the Department of Defense [DOD], DHS) to identify a pool of individuals both from within and outside the federal sector who have appropriate level security clearances, as well as the expertise needed to serve as peer reviewers for the program needs. If specific deficiencies in the roster of potential reviewers are identified, the EPA could identify additional experts who then would apply for an appropriate level of security clearance.

- The NHSRC could establish an advisory committee of outside experts to provide independent peer review, with the expectation that the experts could receive security clearance at appropriate levels. By defining a sufficiently broad mix of individuals on this committee, a pool of individuals qualified to provide an appropriate peer review would be available. Other organizations have developed peer review committees in this manner (e.g., DOD, DHS). For example, the National Institutes of Health's (NIH's) National Science Advisory Board for Biosecurity can operate in a classified manner in providing advice to the Secretary of Health and Human Services, the Director of NIH, and others with respect to biosecurity life sciences research (DHS, 2006b).

COMMUNICATING RESULTS

One of the most difficult challenges faced by the EPA and many other organizations is communicating research results and products effectively to those who need them at the time they need them. In a 2003 report, the EPA's Board of Scientific Counselors emphasized that communicating or disseminating research results is an integral part of the implementation of applied research and requires planning from the outset (EPA, 2003a). This kind of planning involves identifying (1) key audiences; (2) the interests, needs, and concerns of those audiences; and (3) communication methods (e.g., workshops, Web sites, newsletters, documents) that reach the audiences in ways they find useful. In other words, the communications plan should be client-centered.

Recommendations are provided below for improving the NHSRC's water security research communications to complement existing agency initiatives. These recommendations include approaches for identifying the needs of water security stakeholders, improving research synthesis, identifying effective mechanisms for dissemination, evaluating communication strategies, and emphasizing training and technology transfer.

Identifying the Needs of Water Security Stakeholders

The NHSRC should increase its use of formal and informal methods of soliciting early input and involvement from its priority audiences to improve the effectiveness of its research communication and dissemination efforts and products. Some examples include getting input from audiences prior to developing a communication effort, pretesting materials on an intended audience, and soliciting feedback on communication efforts during early phases of implementation. Based on the results of this so-called *formative evaluation*, changes can be made to increase the usefulness and effectiveness of the communication products. The comprehensiveness and rigor of formative evaluation can be adjusted based on the importance, scope, and resources expended on the communication program itself. In the long run, formative evaluation can save resources by ensuring that communication reaches those who most need or want it in ways these audiences find useful (Rossi et al., 2004).

A good example of formative research that may serve as a model for the water sector is the Centers for Disease Control and Prevention's (CDC's) use of qualitative audience research to provide insights into the values, beliefs, and behaviors of the audiences for the National Report on Human Exposure to Environmental Chemicals (CDC, 2003b). The CDC conducted a formative evaluation to identify priority audiences and to develop its communication strategy, messages, and materials. Based on follow-up research, additional ways to further improve communication for subsequent reports were identified.

The success of the EPA's water security research program will be dependent on the ability to supply stakeholders with useful research products in a timely manner. Seven general categories of potential users of published research and technical support information are identified in the Action Plan (EPA, 2004a): water industry representatives, response organizations, public health organizations, federal agencies, laboratories, academia, and the general public. Potential users of the information vary from DHS, which may require highly classified information, to the media and general public. Not all potential users can be identified *a priori*; some potential users may only realize their need for the information at the time of an incident or suspected incident. The EPA should take into account the wide range of audiences for the water security research findings to identify the most effective approaches to disseminate the information. Therefore, a more systematic strategic effort to characterize specific audiences and to identify and prioritize their needs will likely improve the success of information sharing of the EPA's water security research products.

Information Synthesis

Utilities, public health organizations, first responders, and the public look to the EPA's water security research products to help them make decisions about emergency response planning and preparedness, and these users need research products that effectively synthesize the relevant available information. As discussed in Chapter 2, the recent fast pace of security-specific research has led to a flood of focused publications in the scientific literature, and it is a challenge for end users to keep up with the latest findings. Information synthesis is an important element of research translation that can summarize the state of knowledge, highlight the relevance of research findings to end users, and generalize the results, where applicable, to other dual-use applications. Synthesis efforts should be valued and thoughtfully developed in the EPA's continued water security research program to improve the usefulness of its research products. Many Action Plan projects seem to be directed at some level of information synthesis, although it is too early to judge the effectiveness of these products.

Techniques and Outlets for Information Dissemination

The value of research findings can only be realized when people who have the ability to affect change are aware of the information and can access and use the results. The EPA uses its NHSRC Web site[2] and secondarily its Water Security Division Web site[3] as the primary mechanisms to disseminate its nonsensitive water security research findings and technical support products. Through these Web sites, nonclassified documents are available to individuals who seek them. Through Web searches or frequent visits to the Web sites, the water-sector specialist can stay current with newly released scientific reports. However, there are other sector specialists who do not regularly seek out the online documents. Multiple mechanisms exist for making end users aware that new water security research and technical support information is available, including homeland security-specific mechanisms and broadly applicable information portal technology, which are described below.

The EPA faces an additional challenge of information overload when communicating the results of EPA water security research. As noted in

---

[2] *http://www.epa.gov/nhsrc/wip.htm.*
[3] *http://cfpub.epa.gov/safewater/watersecurity/index.cfm.*

Chapter 4, the results of the Action Plan are expected to be released in an estimated 75 different documents, databases, or tools. Not all entities within the water sector will understand the practical relevance or have use for all the information generated for improving water security. The EPA has articulated a desire to make information available widely across the expansive water sector, and the committee encourages this practice. Nevertheless, the EPA could be more effective in its dissemination if it categorized and defined a primary audience for each of its information products (e.g., researchers, public health officials, utilities) and endeavored to disseminate its focused products to specific stakeholder groups. Both security-specific communication mechanisms (e.g., WaterSC, WaterISAC) and portal technology described below can be used to achieve this objective.

Security-Specific Communication Mechanisms

Several communication mechanisms exist, including the Water Information Sharing and Analysis Center (WaterISAC), the Water Security Channel (WaterSC), and the Homeland Security Information Network (HSIN; see Box 2-1), that have the capability of broadcasting nonclassified information to water security stakeholders. Membership in the WaterISAC requires fee-based subscriptions and is limited to water and wastewater utilities, state administrators, and EPA personnel. However, the WaterSC provides free access to a broader range of end users, including academic researchers, public responders, and a larger number of utilities. Once established, the HSIN will also provide access to the same broad suite of users as the WaterSC.

Use of these security-specific mechanisms would enable the EPA to reach out to a large portion of its intended audience and directly notify interested parties about recently published material via e-mail notices. Over the last two years, reaching individual water utilities has become more effective through the use of the WaterISAC and the WaterSC. Not only is urgent information pushed out via e-mail, telephone, and personal digital assistants, but background information useful for security planning, research, and response is stored in the online library. Currently more than 8,000 organizations receive direct notification of available resources. Although 8,000 may seem only a small percentage of U.S. water utilities, the actual number of recipients expands when retransmission of messages is considered. For example, a state primacy agency may transmit an important WaterSC notification it has received to utilities within its state borders. With states currently subscribing to the WaterISAC and local governments affiliating with the WaterSC, important notifications should be further disseminated to very small utilities, assuming that updated contact information can be maintained (D. VanDe Hei, WaterISAC, personal communication, 2006).

The EPA should use these security-specific communication mechanisms to inform affiliates of newly published reports available on the WaterSC, HSIN, or the EPA's Web site. WaterISAC and WaterSC notices can target specific stakeholders and highlight the relevance of the EPA products for these end users. If the EPA embraces this approach, it would need to work with the WaterISAC to help identify the target audiences for its research products and incorporate those stakeholders as affiliates of the WaterSC. The WaterISAC board of managers continues to evaluate the need to expand the WaterISAC user base to include groups such as researchers and consultants to meet their needs to collaborate and share information on important research projects and findings. The WaterISAC is also considering developing linkages to other critical-sector ISACs to improve information sharing with interdependent sectors (D. VanDe Hei, WaterISAC, personal communication, 2006).

Research findings need to be disseminated to the appropriate audiences within the constraints of data sensitivity guidelines. Some of the EPA's water security research, however, will result in information that is either classified or is "for official use only" and therefore will not be distributed widely. Sensitive but unclassified information could be made available to registered users in secure areas such as the WaterISAC. For example, the EPA could work with the WaterISAC to establish a separate area on the Web site for the EPA's sensitive findings and this area could be made accessible only to vetted users who have a demonstrated "need to know." However, the EPA also needs to find ways to "sanitize" important information from classified and sensitive documents so that the main message from the research can be made available to all end users who need it. Even if the final product remains sensitive or classified, the EPA should communicate broadly the nature of the research that has been conducted. In this manner, researchers, public health officials, or others could contact EPA staff to determine if access to the research information should be allowed. While keeping some kinds of information classified or "for official use only" might be reasonable under routine conditions, some mechanism should also be available to release information in emergency situations to an appropriate class of user (e.g., a water utility operator) without requiring a formal security clearance.

Information Portal Technology

Users of the information produced by the NHSRC cannot all be identified *a priori*, because some users may only realize their need for the information during an actual security event. Therefore, the EPA should supplement the above targeted mechanisms with other non-subscription-based mechanisms to disseminate its water security research products. The development of a usable information portal is an effective and essential component of an information sharing strategy, making information easily and readily accessible to the full range of stakeholders.

Merely putting information on a Web site is not sufficient. In the EPA's NHSRC Web site, research materials are organized broadly by topical area, but the site is challenging to navigate and will become more so once many of the research products from the Action Plan are released. The quantity of research information anticipated from the EPA's water security program is so large that special attention is needed to make the information navigable and easily accessible. In addition, the EPA has multiple Web sites on water security, reflecting the efforts of both the Office of Water and the ORD, and the two sites are not well integrated. These multiple access points and the absence of a single, easily navigable portal for water security are certain to confuse and frustrate the casual stakeholder seeking specific information in a timely fashion.

The goal of the water security portal should be to become a primary source for water security research information and a true entry portal for further information of arbitrary depth and specialization. Such sites now exist for other focused interest communities and have become the initial stops for particular topics. Two examples are the federal National Library of Medicine's Web site for the National Center for Biotechnology Information[4] for genomics and bioinformatics information and the private nonprofit Flu Wiki[5] for influenza pandemic resources and information.

The following possible features should be explored in the development of an information portal:

- carefully designed "Frequently Asked Questions" with appropriate subsidiary links;
- predesigned information "tours" targeted toward users at various skill and interest levels (e.g., beginner, intermediate, advanced) with se-

---

[4] *http://www.ncbi.nlm.nih.gov/.*
[5] *http://www.fluwikie.com/.*

lected expository material, links to research products or other sites at the appropriate level, and branched directions for particular interests;

- selected links to other appropriate sites (e.g., Office of Water, DHS, WaterSC) with appropriate annotation describing what can be found there;
- special interest pages (e.g., rumors, subject-filtered news links, trade association links with annotations);
- links to reference sources and relevant texts;
- links to appropriate personnel directories; and
- perhaps an open forum page for the exchange of information.

An effective information portal requires significant advance investment in design followed by a commitment to user testing. It requires dedicated communications staff with expertise in Web design and in human-computer interactions to design, manage, and maintain. An investment in staff is an essential component of making the research products usable, which should be the ultimate objective of the EPA's water security effort. The communication staff should work closely with an advisory committee on information sharing, with representation from existing ISACs, to guide the effort and help it meet the needs of the user community.

Staff dedicated to locating, linking, and situating relevant water security information within the portal site would also have the important function of promoting and enhancing the coordination and information exchange between divisions within EPA, between EPA and other government agencies, and with the private sector. The simple but crucial mechanism of constructing a general water security information portal could help address the problems of lack of coordination and communication, which are significant barriers to efficient use of resources and effective harvesting of useful information.

Evaluating and Improving Communication Strategies

Feedback mechanisms are essential to identify the types of organizations using the EPA's water security research and to learn ways to improve the content and dissemination of the results. With current dissemination mechanisms, the EPA will have difficulty determining the degree to which information is used in security planning, preparedness, and recovery activities in the water sector. Thus, the EPA should develop mechanisms to elicit feedback from the users of its water security products, to learn what information and what products have been especially useful and what improvements may be needed. The EPA should consider using the WaterISAC as one means of soliciting feedback from its subscribers through mechanisms sent directly to the WaterISAC subscribers. Any information portal should also include mechanisms for soliciting feedback from end users.

Technology Transfer and Training

Technology transfer for EPA tools, databases, and computer models is just as important as disseminating products, and training is particularly critical to successful implementation of the research products. Although the EPA has made significant investments in training programs related to some tools (e.g., AT Planner, message mapping, Response Protocol Toolbox), the agency relies heavily upon information technology to provide technology transfer and training. Whether information technology can supplant the need for human interaction should be considered carefully. Short courses and workshops are obviously relatively expensive modes of information delivery. Nevertheless, they provide human interaction that is a vital dimension of information sharing, especially because of the complexity and uniqueness of water security issues. Moreover, the response of attendees can lead to improved products, thus benefiting the EPA's future research program. In particular, short courses and workshops should be developed to support the EPA's water security tools and models when it can be determined that face-to-face interaction adds substantial value over information technology training mechanisms. The EPA's "train-the-trainer" concept, in which the agency trains state water program personnel on drinking water-related issues including water security, has also been effective to facilitate information and technology transfer to local utilities.

Existing nongovernmental organizations also may be able to assist the EPA in transferring information and tools from the arena of research and development to the water utilities and consulting engineers who can benefit from them. Organizations such as the Water Environment Foundation, American Water Works Association, the American Society of Civil Engineers, and the WaterISAC can help relay the availability of important new tools and information to their members. Meanwhile, the EPA should continue to seek new partners (e.g., The Infrastructure Security Partnership,[6] the Applied Technology Council[7]) who might help communicate the availability and usefulness of new tools and databases to a broader userbase.

CONCLUSIONS AND RECOMMENDATIONS

With the permanent establishment of the NHSRC, thoughtful research management planning is essential to build a strong long-term program in water security. The following recommendations and conclusions are provided in support of this goal:

The EPA's Water Infrastructure Protection Division should formally articulate its mission and program objectives as it moves beyond the short-term time frame of the Action Plan. To enhance a vision for future research, the committee presents three strategic objectives for organizing future water security research initiatives, emphasizing research products that can guide pre-incident, incident, and post-incident water security activities. Within these objectives, priority setting will be necessary, and several prioritizing criteria are presented. A strategic planning exercise is a logical and necessary extension of the Action Plan that will strengthen the EPA's leadership in the field. Although it is beyond the committee's charge to recommend a specific strategic planning model, the EPA will need to investigate existing planning and decision-making models before embarking on this endeavor to ensure a successful and appropriately inclusive planning process.

The EPA should develop greater in-house research capability, or at least subject matter expertise, in disciplines that have been historically weak at the EPA and where long-term water security concerns are projected. Now that the NHSRC has been made permanent, it should reassess the pros and cons of using contracts as the principal management tool for conducting research in many of the areas the EPA is not currently staffed or equipped to handle. Based on the advantages articulated in this chapter, extramural funding should be used to support

---

[6] The Infrastructure Security Partnership (TISP) is a national public-private partnership promoting collaboration to improve the resilience of the nation's critical infrastructure against the adverse impacts of natural and man-made disasters. For more information, see *http://www.tisp.org*.

[7] The Applied Technology Council's mission is to develop and promote state-of-the-art, user-friendly engineering resources and applications for use in mitigating the effects of natural and other hazards on the built environment. For more information, see *http://www.atcouncil.org*.

some research in the EPA's water security research program. Careful attention, however, should be given to achieving the right balance. Even if research is to be conducted via contracts, the EPA needs adequate in-house expertise to evaluate and manage such contracts. Increased subject area expertise is specifically needed in the areas of physical security, behavioral sciences, and information management.

The NHSRC should explore alternatives to improve independent peer review of sensitive or classified work. A major challenge is independent peer review of NHSRC activities that contain classified, or sensitive but unclassified, material. Effective independent peer review is an important mechanism for avoiding research errors, program problems, and inefficiencies, but currently, sensitive and classified peer-review mechanisms within the NHSRC may not be sufficient. Therefore, the EPA should review areas where independent peer review involving sensitive and classified material is needed and examine available mechanisms for accomplishing peer review, such as those used by other federal agencies.

The NHSRC should solicit early input and involvement from its priority audiences to improve the effectiveness of its research communication. Communication strategies are more likely to be effective if target audiences are asked for input *prior* to the communication effort. This can be accomplished by characterizing specific audiences in advance, getting input from audiences prior to developing a communication effort, pretesting materials on an intended audience, and soliciting feedback on communication efforts during early phases of implementation. These efforts can save resources by ensuring that research communications reach those who most need it in ways the stakeholders will find useful.

The NHSRC should improve its approaches to information dissemination, using both security-specific communication mechanisms and broadly applicable portal technology. The EPA wishes to make its research products widely available to the water sector, and the committee encourages this practice. However, current Web-based approaches to dissemination need to be improved. Use of security-specific mechanisms (e.g., WaterISAC, WaterSC, HSIN) would enable the EPA to reach out to a large portion of its intended audience and facilitate direct notification about recently published material. The EPA should continue to use the WaterISAC to alert stakeholders to the availability of sensitive materials. Because predicting in advance who will need the information produced by the NHSRC is difficult, the EPA should also consider developing a Web-based information portal to make the research findings easily and readily accessible to the full range of stake-holders. Feedback mechanisms should be developed to learn what products have been especially useful and what improvements may be needed. Technology transfer and training activities are also critical to the successful implementation of research products.

The EPA should consider methods to disseminate important but sensitive security information. The EPA should analyze the costs and benefits of keeping information secure and, if necessary, find ways to communicate important information from classified and sensitive research products so that the research can be useful to stakeholders who need it. The EPA should also consider options for releasing classified or "for official use only" information that could improve response and recovery at the time of a water security emergency.

The EPA water security research will only reduce risk if the products are made available to and properly utilized by utilities; local, state, and federal response agencies; and the public. Therefore, the above recommendations on improving communication and addressing information security barriers are critical to the success of the research program and should be the agency's highest priorities.

6

Recommendations for Future Research Directions

Progress has been made in the Environmental Protection Agency's (EPA's) water security research program (see Chapter 4), but many important research questions and technical support needs remain. In Chapter 3, a framework is suggested for evaluating water security research initiatives that gives priority to research that improves response and recovery and/or develops risk reduction or consequence mitigation measures. The research should also produce tools with a reasonable likelihood of implementation and, where feasible, dual-use benefits. Based on this framework and the review of water security efforts already under way, two important water security research gaps are identified and discussed briefly in this chapter. In addition, short- and long-term water security research recommendations are made. The research recommendations are organized in this chapter according to the three long-term program objectives proposed in Chapter 5 emphasizing pre-incident, incident, and post-incident applications: (1) develop products to support more resilient design and operation of facilities and systems, (2) improve the ability of operators and responders to detect and assess incidents, and (3) improve response and recovery. Both drinking water and wastewater research priorities are addressed together within these three objectives to maximize research synergies that may exist.

KEY RESEARCH GAPS

The Water Security Research and Technical Support Action Plan (EPA, 2004a) set out a comprehensive guide for the EPA's near-term research initiatives. Although the Action Plan was intended to provide a short-term (three- to four- year) research agenda, the previous National Research Council review (NRC, 2004) noted that several of the Action Plan projects represented long-term research questions not easily addressed in the original time frame. Therefore, the Action Plan provides a reasonable starting point for building the EPA's future research program. Nevertheless, the short-term planning horizon of the Action Plan prevented consideration of two key subjects that are critical to a long-term water security research program: behavioral science and innovative system design. The committee recommends the EPA work in collaboration with other organizations to build research initiatives in these two areas.

Behavioral Science

The threat of bioterrorism presents new and different types of risks that are dynamic and pose difficult trade-offs, bringing about intellectual challenges and an emotional valence possibly more important than the risks themselves. Developing an effective communication strategy that meets the needs of the broad range of stakeholders (e.g., response organizations, water organizations and utilities, public health agencies, the public, the media) while addressing security concerns is clearly a high-priority research area. The EPA's work on risk communication is focused primarily on the development of guidance, protocols, and training, and little emphasis has been devoted to interdisciplinary behavioral science research to better prepare stakeholders for water security incidents or to build confidence in their ability to respond. Behavioral science research could help address, for example, what the public's beliefs, opinions, and knowledge about water security risks are; how risk perception and other psychological factors affect responses to water-related events; and how to communicate these risks with the public (Gray and Ropeik, 2002; Means, 2002; Roberson and Morely, 2005b). A better understanding of what short-term disruptions customers are prepared to tolerate may also guide response and recovery planning and the development of recovery technologies.

Previous experience with natural disasters and environmental risks provides a basis for investigating and predicting human behavior in risky situations (Fischoff, 2005). Existing models of human behavior during other kinds of crises, however, may not be adequate to forecast human behavior during bioterrorism or water security incidents (DiGiovanni et al., 2003).

Risk communicators consider empirical findings from psychology, cognitive science, communications, and other behavioral and social sciences to varying extents (Bostrom and Lofstedt, 2003). Although decision makers frequently predict panic and irrational behavior in times of crisis, behavioral science researchers have found that people respond reasonably to such challenges (e.g., Fishoff, 2005). Given the urgency of terror risk communication, risk communicators are obliged to incorporate existing behavioral science research as it relates to water security risks.

The EPA should take advantage of existing behavioral science research that may be applicable to water security issues, but this requires knowledge and experience in behavioral science research. Where gaps exist, the EPA will need to engage in interdisciplinary, rigorous empirical research to obtain the necessary knowledge.

Innovative Designs for Secure and Resilient Water and Wastewater Systems

Innovative designs for water and wastewater infrastructure were not addressed in the EPA Action Plan, but the topic deserves a place in a long-term water security research program. The EPA's research mission has traditionally included the development and testing of new concepts, technologies, and management structures for water and wastewater utilities to achieve practical objectives in public health, sustainability and cost-effectiveness. The addition of homeland security to its mission provides a unique opportunity to take a holistic view of current design and management of water and wastewater infrastructures. Innovation is needed to address the problem of aging infrastructures while making new water systems more resilient to natural hazards and malicious incidents. The EPA should, therefore, take a leadership role in providing guidance for the planning, design, and implementation of new, more sustainable and resilient water and wastewater facilities for the 21st century.

Disagreggation of large water and wastewater systems should be an overarching theme of innovation. Large and complex systems have developed in the United States following the pattern of urban and suburban sprawl. While there are clear economies of scale for large utilities in construction and system management, there are distinct disadvantages as well. The complexity of large systems makes security measures difficult to implement and complicates the response to an attack. For example, locating the source of incursion within the distribution system and isolating contaminated sections are more difficult in large and complex water systems. Long water residence times are also more likely to occur in large drinking water systems, and, as a result, disinfectant residual may be lacking in the extremities of the system because of the chemical and biological reactions that occur during transport. From a security perspective, inadequate disinfectant residual means less protection against intentional contamination by a microbial agent.

A breadth of possibilities exists for improving security through innovative infrastructure design. Satellite water treatment plants could boost water quality. Strategic placement of treatment devices (e.g., ultraviolet lamp arrays) within the distribution system could counter a bioterrorism attack. Wastewater treatment systems could be interconnected to provide more flexibility in case of attack, and diversion devices could be installed to isolate contaminants. Box 6-1 describes some of these concepts in greater detail, and specific research recommendations are suggested in the following section.

RESEARCH RECOMMENDATIONS: DEVELOP PRODUCTS TO SUPPORT MORE RESILIENT DESIGN AND OPERATION OF FACILITIES AND SYSTEMS

Specific research topics are suggested here in two areas to support development of more resilient water and wastewater systems: (1) innovative designs for water and wastewater and (2) improved methods for risk assessment, including processes for threat and consequence assessments.

Innovative Designs for Water and Wastewater Systems

Innovative changes to water infrastructure will require long-term investment in research. Existing systems have been in place for more than a century in older cities. Thus, bold new directions will understandably require intensive research at the outset to produce a defensible economic argument for change. On the other hand, the EPA has the opportunity to develop innovative approaches that can be implemented almost immediately in relatively new, as well as planned, urban and suburban areas. The first step in research would be to enumerate the opportunities for innovation, recognizing the constraints brought about by the size, age, and complexity of existing water and wastewater infrastructures. A broad-gauge, economic analysis should follow that would quantify the costs and multiple benefits of these innovative designs (e.g., increased security, improved drinking water quality, enhanced sustainability of water resources). In addition, there is an implicit need for EPA research-

---

BOX 6-1
Envisioning New Water and Wastewater Infrastructures

Three infrastructure concepts illustrate potential innovative approaches for improving the security and resilience of water and wastewater systems: (1) distribution and collection system interventions, (2) the use of distributed networks, and (3) the implementation of dual piping systems. Water distribution system interventions could include multiple points of treatment within the distribution system (e.g., UV disinfection, chemical addition) or effective in-line monitoring and localized diversion, using multiple valves and interconnections for routing contaminated water out of the distribution system network. In wastewater collections systems, new designs might include real-time monitoring, interventions to isolate portions of the collection system should toxic or explosive constituents be detected (e.g., sensor-activated inflatable dams), and interconnections or online storage capacity for diversion, containment, and treatment.

The "distributed optimal technology network" (DOT-Net) concept (Weber, 2002; 2004) includes a holistic approach to decentralization of both water and wastewater treatment. The premise is that advanced water treatment would be installed most economically at the scale of households, apartment complexes, or neighborhoods using POU/POE technology. These devices offer protection against chemical and biological agents that escape conventional water treatment as well as agents that may be added to the distribution system subsequent to treatment. An almost infinite number of Infrastructure variations involving water and wastewater are possible, even including the localized processing of wastewater for energy recovery.

An alternative concept of a dual water distribution system has been proposed to address water quality concerns in aging infrastructures while meeting demand for fire protection (Okun, 1997). Additional benefits could be gained by incorporating satellite and decentralized wastewater treatment facilities. In this concept, the existing water distribution system and storage tanks would be used for delivery of reclaimed water and for fire demand, and a new water distribution system would deliver potable water through much smaller diameter pipes (Snyder et al., 2002). The dual distribution system concept offers several security advantages. For example, fire protection would not depend upon the integrity of the potable water supply in the event of a terrorist attack. The installation of small diameter stainless steel pipes would reduce residence time in the system (and related water quality degradation) and also speed the recovery process from a chemical or biological attack. However, a dual distribution system might also make a contamination attack on the drinking water supply easier because less contaminant mass would be needed to produce a toxic effect.

ers to coordinate with the agency's regulatory branch to validate the feasibility of the innovative concepts that are proposed.

Each of the infrastructure concepts illustrated in Box 6-1 require far more research to become feasible. The recommendations below outline specific research topics that, if addressed, could improve the safety and sustainability of water resources in the 21st century.

Disaggregation of Water and Wastewater Systems

The "distributed optimal technology network" (DOT-Net) concept (Norton and Weber, 2005; Weber, 2002; 2004) hinges upon the feasibility of distributed treatment via point-of-use (POU)/point-of-entry (POE) devices installed at the scale of individual buildings or perhaps small neighborhoods. The corollary premise is that installation of expensive advanced treatment technology at the centralized water treatment facility is unnecessary when only a fraction of the service area outside a "critical radius" requires additional protection. Only a broad economic analysis of this concept has been published thus far for a hypothetical urban center, but the assumptions need to be verified for actual systems, particularly because of the unique characteristics of individual cities. In addition, far more research is needed on the utility management required to ensure the reliability of POU/POE devices in widespread implementation.

Dual water systems have also been proposed to address aging infrastructure (see Box 6-1; Okun, 1997; 2005). As with the DOT-Net concept, long-term research is needed to determine the costs and benefits of constructing an entirely new paradigm for distribution system design. Research issues would include assessing the acceptability of reclaimed water for progressively more intense levels of nonpotable use (e.g., irrigation, toilet flushing, laundering), the acceptability and management demands of decentralized wastewater treatment facilities, and the net benefits to water security.

In-Pipe Interventions to Reduce Exposure

In-pipe engineering interventions (see Box 6-1) are deserving of research in a long-term water security research strategy. For example, research is needed to optimize the location of disinfection booster stations or to examine the effectiveness and feasibility of *in situ* ultraviolet (UV) irradiation systems as a decontamination strategy. EPA research could also examine various pipe materials (e.g., stainless steel) and evaluate their benefits for security and sustainability relative to their costs.

Infrastructure Designs to Enable Isolation and Interconnection

Most large drinking water systems have the ability to isolate portions of their distribution systems during necessary system repairs, but security concerns provide a new impetus for rapid and effective isolation mechanisms. Research on innovative mechanisms to isolate or divert contaminated water in drinking water and wastewater systems would be useful. The EPA should identify these design options, research their costs and benefits (including dual-use benefits) and their feasibility both for existing systems and new infrastructure, and make this information available to system managers.

Improved Risk Assessments Procedures

A sound risk assessment process allows utilities to make better resource management decisions for enhancing their recovery capacity or security strategies to mitigate the consequences of an attack. The risk assessment process includes assessments of threat, consequences, and vulnerability. To date, most of the efforts to guide utilities in their own risk assessments have focused on vulnerabilities.

Threat Assessment

Water and wastewater utilities today are making resource management decisions related to security without adequate information about the nature and likelihood of threats to their systems. As discussed in Chapter 4, the EPA has focused their efforts on identifying contaminant threats without conducting similarly detailed analyses of possible physical and cyber threats. Both the *nature* and *likelihood* of these threats are needed for efficient allocation of resources at the utility level and within the EPA's research program. Improved threat assessment would require the EPA and/or a consortium of water experts to work closely with the intelligence community and local law enforcement agencies. Other national and federal laboratory expertise within the Department of Energy

Department of Defense, and private-public community might be needed as well. Threat assessments for water and wastewater should be periodically reviewed to identify threat scenarios that should be added to the list and to remove those that are no longer a concern. The development of a threat assessment process for local water and wastewater utilities with current techniques used in other infrastructures would also be helpful, provided the threat information could be communicated to those who need it (ASME, 2004; Sandia National Laboratories, 2001).

Consequence Assessment

A consequence assessment should accompany the threat assessment within the risk assessment process. Consequence assessments would provide decision makers with information on the potential for fatalities, public health impacts, economic impacts, property damage, systems disruption, effects on other infrastructures, and loss of public confidence. Procedures for determining the expected consequences from an attack or natural disaster are not currently being systematically developed. As a result, water system managers do not have sufficient data to make decisions about the benefits of risk reduction relative to the costs. The development and application of a consequence assessment procedure would provide decision makers with information needed to decide whether to mitigate the consequences, upgrade with countermeasures, take steps to improve response and recovery capacity, and/or decide to accept the level of risk and take no further action. A fault tree analysis that includes, for example, options for redundant systems or contingency water supplies could provide vital information on whether to invest in security upgrades or less costly consequence mitigation strategies. Many of these approaches have already been developed for other infrastructures (e.g., Risk Assessment Methodology [RAM]-T for the high-voltage power transmission industry or RAM-D for dams, locks, and levees; see Sandia National Laboratories, 2001; 2002). A thorough review of other RAM methodologies could provide guidance for consequence assessment strategies that could be incorporated into the Risk Assessment Methodology for Water Utilities (RAM-W).

The EPA has worked to develop the AT Planner tool to assist utilities in assessing the consequences from physical attacks (see Chapter 4). While AT Planner has been validated against actual blast test data for nonwater systems, there remains significant uncertainty in the applicability of the modeling for water security because it has not been validated against the structures specific to those systems. Therefore, the ongoing evaluation of AT Planner by the EPA and select water utility operators should include an assessment of the applicability of AT Planner for each of the critical and high-consequence components of a water system. The EPA and water utilities should then consider whether any additional validation testing is needed to determine specific failure modes of relevant water system components (e.g., actual storage tanks, pumps, water conduits, chlorine tanks) and possible countermeasures.

Summary of Research Priorities for
Secure and Resilient Systems

Short-Term Priorities

- Develop an improved understanding of physical, cyber, and contaminant threats to water and wastewater systems, especially focusing on physical and cyber threats.
- Communicate information on threats and consequences to water system managers through training and information exchange.
- Develop an improved threat assessment procedure for water and wastewater utilities that will assist local utilities with their security and response planning.
- Develop a process to assist local utilities in determining the consequences from physical, cyber, and contaminant attacks.
- Update the risk assessment methodology for water systems to incorporate the latest approaches used in other industries, including developing credible threat descriptions and identifying cascading consequences.

Long-Term Priorities

- Develop innovative design strategies for drinking water and wastewater systems that mitigate security risks and identify their costs and benefits in the context of public health, sustainability, cost-effectiveness, and homeland security. These designs might include:
  o In-pipe intervention strategies for drinking water systems,

- o   Disaggregation of water and wastewater treatment facilities to achieve dual-use benefits, and
- o   Designs that allow for interconnections and isolation.

- Evaluate the need to validate AT Planner against structures specific to water systems.
- Periodically review the EPA's prioritized list of threats, contaminants, and threat scenarios to identify items that should be added to the list and remove items that are no longer a concern.
- Continue development of technology transfer/training programs so that utilities understand the value of the EPA's products for both homeland security incidents and natural disasters and know how to utilize the tools to their full extent.

Implementation of Priorities

Some of the research recommendations to support more resilient design and operation of drinking water and wastewater systems lie outside of the EPA's traditional areas of expertise. To support the Action Plan efforts so far, the EPA has relied heavily on expert contractors to conduct this type of work. The EPA should continue to seek the relevant expertise of other federal agencies and national laboratories in these future efforts. However, the EPA will need to consider how best to balance intramural and extramural research funding to carry out this research, while maintaining appropriate oversight and input into the research activities (see also Chapter 5). Increasing staff expertise in some key areas, such as physical security, will be necessary to build a strong and well-rounded water security research program to support more resilient system design and operation.

RESEARCH RECOMMENDATIONS: IMPROVE THE ABILITY OF OPERATORS AND RESPONDERS TO DETECT AND ASSESS INCIDENTS

Suggestions are provided in this section for future research that should improve the ability of operators and responders to detect and assess water security incidents. Specific research suggestions in the areas of analytical methodologies and monitoring and distribution system modeling are discussed below.

Analytical Methodologies and Monitoring

Expanding Existing Analytical Methods

For some analytes of relevance to water security concerns, the available or approved detection methods are poor (e.g., some nonregulated analytes). More work needs to be done to expand existing methods to a broader range of analytes. For example, method 300.1 (EPA, 2000) covers only the common anions but could be extended to others, including toxic substances. The extension of existing methods to new analytes would allow a broader range of laboratories to expand their capabilities into the water security area.

Screening methods using conventional gas chromatography (GC) or high-performance liquid chromatography (HPLC) should also be investigated. Modern high-resolution chromatography combined with high-sensitivity detection (e.g., electron capture, fluorescence) is a powerful, yet accessible tool. Protocols should be developed to make the best use of these widely available capabilities. Software will have to be developed to facilitate the documentation of normal, background signals (fingerprint-type chromatograms). This background information can then be used to detect anomalies. Final protocols would have to be tested thoroughly against priority chemical contaminants. Chromatographic fingerprints have been used to monitor water supplies for nonintentional contamination, so this line of research would provide a dual benefit (D. Metz, Ohio River, personal communication, 2006; P. Schulhof, Seine River, personal communication, 2006).

Progress is being made with the protocol to concentrate samples and identify biological contaminants by polymerase chain reaction (PCR) analysis. Continued research, however, needs to be directed towards reducing the time and effort required to collect, process, and identify samples by automating portions of the protocol such as the concentration step. Such automated collection and sample processing systems would be especially valuable in response to security threats, when water samples could be channeled to existing or new detection technologies capable of onsite processing. The EPA should continue to expand the number of biothreat agents tested with the concentration/PCR protocol to include microbes other than spores, prioritizing test organisms that are both a threat to public health and resistant to chlorine (Morales-Morales, et al., 2003; Straub and Chandler, 2003). Continued testing of the concentration/PCR protocol should include various mixed suspensions of a target microbe and background microbes to determine specificity of detection and various dilutions of the target microbe to determine sensitivity of detection. The protocol should also be tested on chloraminated water samples.

Developing New Monitoring Technologies

Chemical Detection. New chemical monitoring technologies for security-relevant analytes should be investigated. Examples include quartz crystal microbalance (QCM) sensors, microfluidic devices (lab-on-a-chip), ion-sensitive field-effect transistors (ISFETs), and larger-scale optrodes. Extramural agency and corporate partnerships developed by the EPA and longer-term research projects will help the evaluation and consideration of a broader range of detection platforms.

Biological Detection. Biological monitoring devices are essential to assess the type and extent of contamination in a suspected water security event. A broader range of innovative and developing detection technologies for biological agents, including methods that are field deployable and reagent-free, should be considered and evaluated. Innovative, field-deployable detection technologies (e.g., genetic fingerprinting, immunodetection, other technologies in development by universities, the Department of Defense, and industry) could reduce the time and effort for detection and enable earlier response efforts (Iqbal et al., 2000; Ivnitski et al., 2003; Lim et al., 2005; Monk and Walt, 2004; Yu and Bruno, 1996; Zhu et al., 2004). These new technologies might also increase the accuracy of detecting deliberate contamination events and reduce false alarms. Methods that can detect multiple biological agents and those with dual-use benefits should be emphasized over those methods limited to very specific agents (Peruski and Peruski, 2003; Rogers and Mulchandani, 1998). For example, DNA fingerprinting might be more useful than immunodetection systems dependent on a highly specific antibody for operation. The accuracy of these detection methods will depend on availability of quality reagents such as antibodies and primers; therefore, researchers will need to work closely with the Centers for Disease Control and Prevention (CDC) and other agencies that have access to such reagents.

Monitoring Devices for Wastewater Collection Systems. Contamination incidents have the potential to disrupt wastewater biological treatment systems; thus, a long-term research program should also include research on monitoring technologies relevant to wastewater security concerns. Although a number of devices are available that can be used to monitor physical, chemical, and biological parameters, none of the currently available devices are robust or reliable enough when used in untreated wastewater to meet security requirements. The EPA should, therefore, encourage development of robust or reliable monitoring devices for wastewater infrastructure.

Syndromic Surveillance Tools. Syndromic surveillance tools may have the potential for detecting disease outbreaks and for investigating the possible role of water in such outbreaks (Berger et al., 2006). The EPA is already working to test two syndromic disease surveillance tools (RODS, ESSENCE) against prior water contamination outbreak data. There are substantive research needs that should be undertaken, however. Clearly, the improvement of existing syndromic surveillance tools is a long-term research objective. For syndromic surveillance to become worthwhile, it should achieve a favorable cost-benefit ratio considering the costs of false positives, and syndromic surveillance should also be adequately integrated into response plans. The implementation of syndromic surveillance systems on a large scale would require a more detailed linkage between disparate databases used in the public health sector and the water supply sector. Research to develop tools to allow local systems to readily fuse information from these disparate sources would be desirable. Such linkages would improve detection and response to waterborne disease outbreaks and more rapidly exclude water as a possible vehicle of disease. This would have important applications for both intentional and nonintentional water contamination events.

Real-Time Monitoring Systems

The development of a fully functional, easy-to-maintain, real-time monitoring system (RTMS) that could someday be used to prevent harm from deliberate attacks on the water system ("detect to prevent"), even with substantial research investments, is many years away. Therefore, the primary emphasis of future research on RTMSs, at least in the near term, should be on developing these technologies to assess the spread of contaminants, not to prevent exposure.

The committee also questions the likelihood of implementation of real-time monitoring devices for specific chemical or biological parameters that are not useful in the day-to-day operation of a system (see Chapters 2 and 4). However, there are a few scenarios where implementation of continuous monitors for biological contaminants might be valuable, such as their use in certain water systems under heightened threat conditions (e.g., utilities for which specific intelligence information indicates they may be targeted). As discussed in Chapter 4, deployment under these circumstances has a greater likelihood for success because the probability of an event is estimated to be much higher and the length of monitoring time is shortened. The use of highly sensitive and specific detection devices under such targeted circumstances would significantly lower the probability of false alarms and reduce the problem of poor positive predictive value (see Chapter 2) while also minimizing implementation and maintenance costs. Thus, improving monitoring systems for specific chemical or biological agents in drinking water is a valid long-term research goal. The EPA may find that longer-term research on more speculative sensor development could benefit from a further broadening of the circle of collaborators. Such speculative research may be more appropriately funded through the National Science Foundation or the Homeland Security Advanced Research Projects Agency, thus freeing up EPA resources for other purposes. To encourage such research, the EPA may wish to build its connections with the private sector on this technology.

Research on detection methods for RTMSs should proceed with careful consideration of the likelihood of implementation of the monitoring devices. In its near-term research plans, the EPA should adopt a first-stage approach to RTMSs, emphasizing generic sensors to detect intrusion or a system anomaly. The intrusion detection would then trigger more resource-intensive follow-up monitoring and analysis. Such an approach has significant dual-use benefits for routine contamination events that could outweigh the costs of implementing and operating these systems. Additional effort to develop cheaper, more accurate, and more easily deployable and maintainable sensors for routine water quality parameters would be useful both for anomaly detection and routine operation. Additional research is also needed, even in first-stage RTMSs, to understand normal water quality variations and distinguish variations that might be caused by a deliberate contamination attack. For example, continuous monitoring of chlorine residual at multiple points in the distribution system often reveals wide variations at different temporal scales due to changes in water demand that affect water residence time (e.g., operation of storage tanks). Although some work to understand inherent water quality variability in distribution systems is being conducted through the

Water Sentinel program, a significant amount of work is needed to translate the findings of this research into criteria for RTMSs to develop systems that have a reasonable likelihood of implementation.

An important component of RTMS research should include data fusion, whereby multiple anomalies must occur before an alarm signal is sent (see also Chapter 4). The private sector seems to be taking the lead on many types of multiparameter approaches to RTMSs and the processing of data, especially as described by contaminant or event signatures. It is important that the algorithms are open to peer review and can be accessed by all for development of new and refined approaches.

RTMS sensor research should consider a broader range of technologies, including full-spectrum UV and visible absorption, fluorescence excitation emission matrices, and ionization sensors (Alupoaei et al., 2004; Fenselau and Demirev, 2001; Lay, 2001). Many of these techniques are used as nonspecific chromatography detectors, and as such, they are highly sensitive. Most prototype RTMSs are composed of existing sensors that are designed to measure a specific contaminant, and some technologies have been excluded because they have not led to sensors with a high degree of selectivity. However, RTMSs need not be contaminant-specific; they only need to detect anomalies. Detection of an anomaly can then be followed by more specific contaminant analyses.

The problem of false positive signals from real-time contaminant-specific warning systems has been discussed in Chapter 2. In essence, the problem is one of unfavorable arithmetic when the probability of a true positive is very small, as it would be for an intentional contamination attack on any particular water system of the tens of thousands of such systems. Therefore, most contaminant-specific alarm signals will be false positives. The EPA should consider the consequences of various rates of false positive signals for both large and small utilities and collect information on how alarms are currently handled by utilities. Workshops and structured surveys on this issue would provide valuable information on current practices, the extent to which positive signals are confirmed, the costs of false alarms, and the views of utility operators on their tolerance for various levels and types of false alarms. This research would provide useful guidance for the developers of water quality monitoring devices, for utilities that are considering implementing devices that are commercially available, and for local and state regulatory agencies who will need assistance interpreting alarm signals in light of the public health consequences.

Technology Testing

The EPA has developed a rigorous technology testing program to provide security product guidance to end users focusing on monitoring and decontamination technology. However, as noted in Chapter 4, the number of relevant security technologies and agents of interest exceed the capacity and budget of the Technology Testing and Evaluation Program (TTEP). Therefore, developing a test-prioritization plan for TTEP seems especially important and is strongly recommended. Although the process of identifying technologies of interest has begun through the use of stakeholder meetings and advisory boards, activities to date have been weighted toward doing the easiest things first, and only some of these tests provided dual-use benefits. Balancing the homeland security benefits and the benefits to routine water system operations in TTEP will likely require additional strategic planning. One strategy has been to test equipment that is commercially available regardless of whether it addresses a high-risk agent. Instead, the EPA should look beyond the easy-to-identify commercially available equipment and make a greater effort to identify technologies in development that have the potential to address those agents identified as posing the greatest risk to water, considering the likelihood of the threat (including the ease of acquiring particular chemical or biological agents), the potential consequences, and the likelihood of implementing the technology. For a few of the highest-priority threats, the EPA may wish to consider providing technical support and/or funding to encourage more rapid development of a particularly promising technology that has a high likelihood of implementation and significant dual-use benefits, similar to the EPA Superfund Innovative Technology Evaluation (SITE) Emerging Technology Program.

Develop Laboratory Capability and Capacity

Adequate laboratory capacity is critical for responding to a terrorist incident affecting water supplies, and although this is not a research issue, the EPA has much to contribute from an applied perspective. The need for mobile analysis units capable of supplementing local laboratories and rapidly responding to geographical areas impacted by terrorist events should be considered. Such mobile laboratories could also address analytical needs that arise during natural catastrophes, such as Hurricane Katrina. Many states have begun to develop mobile laboratory capabilities as part of their water security activities, and the EPA could glean information on their experiences to date.

The EPA is working with utilities and state and federal agencies to build a national laboratory response network for water sample analysis (i.e., the Water Laboratory Alliance). Some university laboratories may have capabilities that could merit inclusion in the nationwide network. Other laboratories may be stimulated to conduct additional research on improved analytical methods for toxic and biothreat agents if they were better informed of the current state of knowledge and had access to reference standards (access to some reference standards is currently limited due to security concerns). To be successful, a dual-use philosophy should be adopted whenever possible in the development of laboratory capacity (e.g., employing methods/instruments that can also be used for standard analytes).

Distribution System Modeling Tools

Distribution system models provide valuable tools for locating the source of contamination or assessing the spread if the source is known, estimating exposure, identifying locations for sampling, and developing decontamination strategies (see also Chapter 4). Distribution system models also have important dual-use applications to routine water quality concerns, and the EPA should continue to emphasize the dual-use value of its modeling tools. Specific recommendations are provided below to advance the capabilities and implementation of the Threat Ensemble Vulnerability Assessment (TEVA) and EPANET models.

Experimental Verification of Species Interaction Subcomponent Models

The final goal of producing a more flexible EPANET model through Multi-Species EPANET (MS-EPANET) is commendable. However, the new subcomponents are based upon developing better fundamental knowledge of reactions within the distribution system involving chemistry (e.g., disinfection kinetics, chemical partitioning), biology (e.g., development of biofilms, release and attachment of microbes), and materials science (e.g., corrosion of pipe materials and its relationship to disinfection efficacy). The large number of system constants in both MS-EPANET and TEVA necessitate significant investment in sensitivity analysis research to quantify the accuracy of model predictions. The development and testing of all new features of MS-EPANET should be a long-term research goal. Until the validity of these subcomponents is verified and system constants can be assigned with more certainty, the water industry will be reluctant to use the full capability of MS-EPANET. Limitations in the accuracy of model predictions will need to be addressed in guidance to decision makers. A significant commitment will be needed in resources for experimental verification.

Alternate Approaches to Uncertainty Modeling

The Action Plan acknowledges correctly that the distribution system model simulations should incorporate an analysis of uncertainty because the point of attack is unknown. This has led to the use of the well-known Monte Carlo analysis to randomize the location of the attack and run repeated distribution system model simulations (1,000 or more) to generate a probability distribution to relate point of attack to human exposure impact. The focus on short-term results, however, has produced weaknesses in the current EPA approach to uncertainty research.

A broader discussion about how to incorporate uncertainty into the TEVA model should be invited. Approaches such as fuzzy logic (McKone and Deshpande, 2005) and Bayesian Maximum Entropy modeling (Serre and Christakos, 1999) are showing promise but have been applied mainly to homogenous space rather than to network domains. The EPA should encourage alternative ideas for handling uncertainty. If the expertise is not available within the agency, there needs to be a mechanism to expand extramural support for research, particularly within th university community.

Transfer and Training in Use of the TEVA and
lels

the TEVA model add significant complexity to the which may limit its widespread implementation. The to communicate the capabilities of EPANET, MS-\ to utilities, emphasizing their value for routine wadvanced homeland security planning, and contami-1 response activities. Until TEVA and MS-ʼveloped and widely available, the EPA should consider an interim strategy to better inform water utilities on the value and use of existing distribution system models, such as EPANET. Progressive water utilities are already using EPANET to examine possible locations of attack and to track the concentration of contaminants within the distribution system.

Training in the use of MS-EPANET and the proposed TEVA model is also needed. Water utility managers need to be convinced that the costs for adapting a new model for their respective distribution systems are worthwhile, because many utilities have already invested heavily in development, verification, and calibration of existing models. The complexity of the TEVA model may increase these costs further, because many more implementation steps follow those for EPANET to adapt the TEVA "template" to the specifics of each water utility.

Summary of Research Priorities for Better Equipping Operators to Detect and Assess Incidents

Short-Term Priorities

Analytical Methodologies and Monitoring

- Automate the concentration step of the concentration/PCR protocol.
- Continue to test the concentration/PCR protocol:
    - o Expand the number of biothreat agents tested to four or five organisms that include microbes other than spores, focusing on microbes that are both a threat to public health and resistant to chlorine.
    - o Test the concentration/PCR protocol with chloraminated water samples.
    - o Test the concentration/PCR protocol to determine sensitivity and specificity of detection.
- Field-test RTMSs to determine false positive/false negative rates and maintenance requirements and develop basic criteria for the technology that might lead to a reasonable likelihood of implementation.
- Continue research to develop a first-stage RTMS based on routine water quality sensors with dual-use applications.

- Analyze the consequences of false positive signals from real-time monitoring systems, emphasizing current practices, the extent to which positive signals are confirmed, the costs of false alarms, and the tolerance of utility operators for false alarms.
- Test standard chromatographic methods for their ability to screen for a broad range of toxic agents in routine laboratory testing.
- Develop a test-prioritization strategy for TTEP to optimize the resources devoted to this effort.

Distribution System Modeling Tools

- Invite external peer review of the TEVA model before investing in field testing.

Long-term Priorities

Analytical Methodologies and Monitoring

- Continue to develop portable, field-deployable systems that can be used to collect and process samples at event locations.
- Formulate protocols and develop software for using GC- and HPLC-based fingerprinting to detect suspicious anomalies.
- Stimulate research and ultimately development of new sensors for water security analytes based on innovative technologies, such as QCM, ISFETS, and microfluidics.
- Evaluate and develop new field-deployable detection technologies for biological agents, including genetic fingerprinting, immunodetection, and reagentless technologies, that have the necessary sensitivity, specificity, and multiplex capabilities.
- Develop improved, cheaper, and accurate RTMSs for routine water quality measurements.
- Examine the use of nonspecific detection technologies for RTMSs.
- Develop data fusion approaches for RTMSs that can minimize false positives.
- Develop and test new monitoring technologies suitable for wastewater security applications.
- Improve syndromic surveillance tools and develop a health surveillance network with appropriate linkages to water quality monitoring.

- Continue to develop and refine the efficiency of a system-wide laboratory response network, including the development of mobile analysis units.

Distribution System Modeling Tools

- Continue fundamental research to understand the chemical and biological reactions that affect the fate and transport of contaminants in distribution systems to verify the constants used in MS-EPANET and TEVA.
- Include alternative approaches to uncertainty design (e.g., fuzzy logic, Bayesian Maximum Entropy) in the TEVA model that are based more strongly upon stochastic than deterministic principles given that many of the input parameters to the current TEVA model are highly uncertain.
- Develop projects for training water utilities in the value and use of EPANET, MS-EPANET, and TEVA.

Implementation of Priorities

Some of these research priorities may be more appropriately accomplished by universities, companies, or other agencies that have the necessary expertise, resources, and funding to successfully complete these tasks. The development of multiplex detection protocols and portable, field-deployable platforms are examples of tasks that might be better managed by some group other than the EPA. Work to determine the sensitivity and specificity of designated protocols for different biothreat agents could be conducted by university laboratories or private industry, with collaborative input from the EPA, considering their understanding of the needs of the water sector. Utilization of research resources outside the EPA would expand the variety of emerging, innovative analytical technologies that might be used to support the EPA's efforts in enhancing the nation's water security.

RESEARCH RECOMMENDATIONS: IMPROVED
RESPONSE AND RECOVERY

Recommendations are provided in this section for future research that should improve response and recovery after a water security incident. Research suggestions related to tools and data for emergency planning and response, contingencies, risk communication and behavioral sciences, decontamination, and lessons learned from natural disasters are presented below.

Tools and Data for Emergency Planning and Response

Continued Development of Emergency Response Databases

The EPA released preliminary versions of the Water Contamination Information Tool (WCIT) and the Consequence Assessment Tool (CAT) to provide data on contaminant properties, toxicity, and exposure threats (see Chapter 4), but the databases are still in their infancy, and numerous data gaps exist. The EPA will need to prioritize its continued efforts to further develop these response databases. Therefore, the EPA should develop strategic plans for WCIT and CAT, outlining the long-term goals for the databases and addressing questions such as:

- What stakeholders will be served by the databases?
- What categories of information do these stakeholders need?
- How many contaminants should be included?
- What linkages to other databases should be established?

The EPA will need to determine criteria for prioritizing what contaminants are added to the database and how to maintain and update the information. If WCIT and CAT are not continually revised to incorporate the latest scientific knowledge, the databases will become outdated. Expanding or even maintaining a database requires considerable resources, both intellectual and financial. If a commitment is not made initially for the necessary resources to update and maintain a database, spending the resources to create it becomes debatable. The EPA is currently facing similar issues maintaining its Integrated Risk Information System (IRIS) database.

The EPA should also clearly define the data quality objectives for WCIT/CAT and incorporate peer review of the data, as necessary, to meet these objectives. For example, the EPA may decide that some information about a contaminant is better than none, even if that information has limitations. This is a legitimate approach; however, the EPA should provide a mechanism that helps to ensure that individuals using the databases understand the data quality and their limitations. One mechanism for accomplishing this would be to add quality notations for each datum. Regardless of the approach taken, the EPA needs to describe the extent to which the data have been reviewed.

Evaluation and Improvement of Tools and Databases

With the forthcoming completion of at least the first stages of many tools and databases (e.g., WCIT, CAT), the EPA should consider the evaluation/improvement cycle. This will require the development of procedures to evaluate the utility and usability of these tools by potential constituencies. In addition, the EPA should take advantage of the tests afforded in response to "real-life" incidents. For example, some of the tools and databases were used (albeit in an early stage of their development) in the response to Hurricane Katrina. A formal assessment of knowledge gained from this experience could assist in the improvement and development of the tools.

Filling Data Gaps

The state of knowledge of the health risks from water contaminants that could be used in a malicious event is quite limited, as shown by the limited number of chemicals and even fewer biologicals in the WCIT/CAT databases and the many blank data fields in these databases. Important experimental and computational research is under way at the EPA to address some of these data gaps (see Chapter 4, Section 3.6), but many gaps remain. There are two applications of toxicity/infectivity information that would be useful to the EPA for response and recovery efforts. The first is development of guidance for dissolved concentrations that would pose an immediate acute risk to exposed individuals, analogous to the inhalation immediate danger to life and health values of the National Institute for Occupational Safety and Health. The EPA is currently working on this problem by developing a database on acute and chronic health effects associated with priority contaminants, although much work remains to be done. The second is guidance for determining the appropriate "acceptable" level remaining after cleanup/decontamination. This second aspect has not yet been strongly emphasized in the EPA research program. It is recommended that the EPA convene a working group to develop research and prioritization strategies for filling these data gaps and for ascertaining current gaps in knowledge with respect to rapid estimation of toxicity/infectivity in the absence of specific experimental information. Decisions for setting priorities for the data gathering efforts should be made with full consideration of dual-use benefits.

Contingencies for Water System Emergencies

Further study of water supply alternatives should be a high priority, considering their pivotal role in response and recovery and their dual-use applications for natural disasters or system failures. However, the subject of water supply contingencies seems to have been given a low priority in the EPA's research program to date. Completion of the work in progress should be the first priority. The committee debated the value of investing significant resources in developing technologies that could supply drinking water for large communities over long-term disruptions because of the rarity of the need for such technologies. Nevertheless, the EPA should draw upon the research and development efforts of the Department of Defense in this area and work to test the application of these technologies to water security scenarios.

The EPA should consider including new research on contingencies for failures of the human subsystem in water system security. Such research could examine current practices for identifying back-up operators in the case of widespread incapacitation in both short-term and long-term scenarios. This research could also identify best practices, which could be incorporated into EPA guidance to water utilities for their emergency response planning.

Preliminary research suggests that geographic information systems (GIS) could be of significant value to utilities for identifying contingencies in the event of system failures. Therefore, further efforts may be needed to inform utilities about the value of GIS for emergency response and provide guidance for integrating GIS into their emergency planning procedures. National geodata standards may be needed to promote consistency and facilitate data exchange among users.

Behavioral Sciences and Risk Communication

The National Homeland Security Research Center (NHSRC) has made substantial progress in the development of risk communication guidance and training (see Chapter 4), but very little emphasis has been devoted to research on understanding how the public may respond to risk communication messages and how to improve communication of risks to the public. Terrorism presents risks that are new, evolving, and difficult to characterize; thus, water security poses communication challenges that should be addressed using scientifically rigorous research in the fields of risk communication and behavioral sciences. The EPA should continually reassess the role risk communication has in its overall risk management framework and fully integrate risk communication efforts into the overall risk management program. Behavioral science and associated risk communication research should be a high priority in the EPA's future water security research plans. The following recommendations are targeted toward water-security events, but the proposed research has dual benefits for improving non-security-related communications with the public.

Analysis of Factors that Build Trust and Improve Communication

Research and experience prove that one of the most important keys to communication success is an organization's ability to establish, maintain, and increase trust and credibility with key stakeholders, including employees, regulatory agencies, citizen groups, the public, and the media. To improve overall communication strategies in a water-related emergency, research is needed that analyzes factors that build trust and reduce fear (e.g., What types of concerns do people have related to public health emergencies, water security issues, or bioterrorism? How do utilities build trust and credibility with the public around water security incidents?). In addition, research is needed to analyze methods to counter and reduce the possibility of misinformation or false information being distributed to the public and key stakeholders.

Understanding Institutional Behavior

Building response and recovery capacity requires agencies that might be involved in a water security event to develop stronger working relationships. Although water utilities, public health agencies, law enforcement, emergency responders, and the media do not have a long history of collaborating and working together, several state drinking water programs have taken the lead in carrying out tabletop exercises as well as on-the-ground exercises to address this issue. These state programs have also undertaken measures to facilitate an understanding of the roles and responsibilities of the various potential players, including federal, state, and local law enforcement; state and local health agencies; state and local emergency response agencies; and water utilities. The EPA could glean useful information from these ongoing state and local activities. Nevertheless, additional research is needed to better understand the culture of the agencies that will be responding to events, how these agencies will interact in a water-related crisis, and what level of effort is needed to maintain collaboration in planning and preparedness. This research could identify barriers to more effective collaboration, and these findings could be used to create training scenarios that could improve coordination and resolve potential conflicts in advance. This research is a short-term priority given the importance of coordinated interaction during a crisis. The research could be performed relatively quickly because there is a wealth of experiences, particularly at the state level, related to agency interactions in water-related crises.

Investigate Applicability of Research in Behavioral Science

While some of the recommended research on risk communication and behavioral science may need to be managed by the EPA to address specific water security-related issues, the EPA should also take advantage of other behavioral science research currently being conducted through university-based partnerships, including those established by the Homeland Security Centers of Excellence program. For example, the University of Maryland's National Consortium for the Study of Terrorism and Responses to Terror (START) is conducting original research on issues that are poorly understood, including risk perception and communication, household and community preparedness for terrorist attacks, likely behavioral responses by the public, social and psychological vulnerability to terrorism, and strategies for mitigating negative psychological effects and enhancing resilience in the face of the terror threat. The START center is also synthesizing existing research findings in order to provide timely guidance for decision makers and the public, paying special attention to how diverse audiences react to and are affected by threats and preparedness efforts.

In addition, the CDC has developed a national network of 50 Centers for Public Health Preparedness (CPHP) to train the public health workforce to respond to threats to our nation's health, including bioterrorism. These centers work to strengthen terrorism preparedness and emergency public health response at the state and local level and to develop a network of academic-based programs contributing to national terrorism preparedness and emergency response capacity. Information from the CPHP may be relevant and useful to the water sector.

Pretesting Risk Communication Messages

Although the message mapping workshops are a good start to assist stakeholders in preparing messages that will be relevant in a water security incident, the messages have not been tested and evaluated. Therefore, the EPA should engage the research community in pretesting messages being developed by the Center for Risk Communication so that case studies and scenarios can be analyzed for effectiveness in reaching key audiences, and problems can be corrected in advance. Sophisticated evaluation techniques and standard research procedures are used by the CDC to pretest public messages. This evaluation research should be based on standard criteria established in the risk communication literature (e.g., Mailback and Parrott, 1995; National Cancer Institute, 2002; Witte et al., 2001).

Analysis of the Risks and Benefits of Releasing Security Information

The decision of when to release or withhold water security information is critical to the development of a risk communication strategy. Therefore, the EPA should analyze the risks and benefits of releasing water security information, considering input from its broad range of constituents, and develop transparent agency guidance on when to release information versus when to withhold it due to security concerns.

The committee considers this a priority because of the difficulty and importance of the information sharing problem.

Water-Related Risk Communication Training

As the lead U.S. agency in water system security, the EPA should assume the responsibility for developing a national training program on water-related risk communication planning and implementation for water managers. This should be done in collaboration with the water and wastewater organizations, state government agencies, public health officials, health care officials, and others engaged in communication of risks during water-related emergencies.

Decontamination

Decontamination research is critical to improving response and recovery, and the products are applicable to address unintentional contamination events from natural disasters (e.g., hurricanes, floods, earthquakes) and routine malfunctions (e.g., pipe breaks, negative pressures due to power losses). The EPA has numerous ongoing projects in this area that should be completed, but additional research topics are also suggested below.

Addressing Data Gaps

EPA decontamination research products released thus far have shown that fundamental physical, chemical, and/or biological characteristics of many threat agents of concern are not yet known. Therefore, additional laboratory research is needed related to the behavior of contaminants in water supply and wastewater systems and methods for decontaminating water infrastructure. For example, one research priority would be to develop inactivation rate data for all microbes of concern with both free and combined chlorine strategies, because both approaches are used in the water industry. Rate and equilibrium data for adsorption/desorption of contaminants on pipe walls is also needed, although the EPA could also take advantage of existing databases on structure-activity relationships to predict these behaviors. Long-term research, perhaps in partnership with other Office of Research and Development units, could enhance our understanding of the fate, transport, and transformation of toxics in water and wastewater environments.

Decontamination Strategies

The EPA should build on its ongoing work in the area of decontamination and address gaps in the current knowledge base. For example, research is needed to examine readily available household inactivation methods for biological agents (including spore-formers), such as microwaving. The EPA should also work to further the development of innovative decontamination technologies that address important water security concerns. Research and development on new POU/POE technologies, such as superheated water devices, could help overcome operational disadvantages of the products currently on the market.

Prioritizing Future Surrogate Research

Surrogates are relevant to numerous water security research applications, including research on contaminant fate and transport, human exposure risks, and decontamination. Research is ongoing to identify surrogates or simulants for biological agents, to determine which surrogates are appropriate, and to determine the ability of typical drinking water disinfection practices (chlorination and chloramination) to inactivate those agents (see Chapter 4, Section 3.2). Much of the research has focused on *Bacillus anthracis* and other bacterial agents, but the EPA should determine if surrogates for research on biotoxins and viruses are needed and whether additional surrogates are needed for other bacterial agents. A viral simulant or surrogate would be helpful to examine virus survival in fresh water, drinking water, and sewage, as well as virus susceptibility to water disinfectants. Research in this area has relevance to viral bioterrorism agents and also has strong dual-use research applications because viral surrogates could facilitate risk assessment studies on natural viruses (e.g., SARS, avian influenza).

Surrogate research is a laborious experimental process (see Box 4-1) that must be conducted in one of the few laboratories already authorized to keep and work with select agents. Considerable research is required to compare the select agent with candidate surrogates under the experimental conditions of interest. As discussed in Chapter 4, surrogates need not mimic in all respects the agents they stand in for. For some important security or decontamination uses, it may only be necessary that they provide an appropriate bound on the characteristic of interest in the target agent (e.g., persistence, disinfectant sensitivity). Therefore, the EPA should carefully consider and prioritize the agents and the research applications for which surrogates are needed. The prioritization process for surrogates should consider the following:

- Which types of research could be greatly facilitated through the availability of surrogates?
- Which types of research with surrogates might have "dual-use" applications (i.e., could the properties of certain surrogates also be usefully extrapolated to other common organisms)?
- Which types of research should be done only with select agents?
- How closely should the surrogate properties of interest match that of the target organism?
- What are the costs and benefits to the research program associated with surrogate development versus use of the pathogenic agents?

The EPA should engage a limited number of individuals (e.g., federal partners, academics) who are involved in similar research in this prioritization process.

Lessons Learned from Natural Disasters

Midway through the committee's work, NRC (2005; see Appendix A) suggested the EPA take advantage of experience gained in the aftermath of Katrina so as to improve future response and recovery efforts for water security. While a hurricane caused this catastrophe, it is conceivable that a similar result might have occurred if the levees had been destroyed by terrorist explosives. Thus, New Orleans offered a living laboratory to study many aspects of the impacts of a disaster on water and wastewater systems of all sizes. Failure modes, infrastructure interdependencies, decontamination and service restoration strategies, the availability of alternative supplies, communication strategies, and the ability to service special institutions (e.g., hospitals) and special needs individuals could all have been examined in the immediate aftermath of the hurricane. To the best of the committee's knowledge, however, the EPA has not attempted to compile a knowledge base from this experience. As time passes, it will become increasingly difficult to reconstruct what transpired. Other natural or manmade disasters, such as the earthquakes in California in 1989 and 1994 or the "Great Flood of 1993" in the Midwest, or natural contamination events, such as the Milwaukee *Cryptosporidium* outbreak, may also offer opportunities to mine important data about the failure or recovery of water and wastewater systems, but detailed information on these earlier occurrences may be lacking. In the future, the NHSRC should be poised to seize opportunities for learning about response and recovery after major natural or man-made disasters affecting water or wastewater systems.

Summary of Research Priorities for Improving Response and Recovery

Short-Term Priorities

Tools and Data for Emergency Planning and Response

- Determine strategic plans for managing and maintaining the WCIT/CAT databases, considering the likely uses and long-term goals for the databases.
- Develop and implement a strategy for evaluating the utility and usability of the response tools and databases, including stakeholder feedback and lessons learned during their use under "real-life" incidents.
- Convene a working group to develop research strategies for filling the data gaps in WCIT/CAT and other planned emergency response databases.

Contingencies for Water Emergencies

- Complete the work in progress on contingencies and infrastructure interdependencies under Section 3.5 of the Action Plan.
- Test and evaluate the most promising innovative water supply technologies that enable or enhance the short- or long-term delivery of drinking water in the event of systemic failure of water systems. Analyze the positive features and those areas needing improvement prior to full-scale deployment.
- Conduct research on potential contingencies for failures of the "human subsystem."

Behavioral Sciences and Risk Communication

- Analyze factors that build trust, reduce fear, and prevent panic to improve overall communication strategies in a water-related emergency.
- Investigate the behavioral science research being conducted by the Homeland Security University Centers of Excellence and other federal agencies for applicability to the water sector.
- Pretest messages being developed by the Center for Risk Communication and analyze case studies and scenarios for effectiveness.
- Analyze the risks and benefits of releasing security information to inform the EPA's risk communication strategies and its practices on information sharing.
- Fully integrate risk communication efforts into the overall risk management program and provide adequate resources that ensure these efforts remain a high priority in the EPA's future water security research program.
- Conduct research to better understand how agencies will interact in a water-related crisis situation and determine what strategies will be most effective in encouraging and maintaining collaboration in planning and preparedness.

Decontamination

- Complete the many decontamination projects in progress under Section 3.4 of the Action Plan.
- Develop predictive models or laboratory data for inactivation of bioterrorism agents in both free chlorine and chloramines that can be used in MS-EPANET and the TEVA model.
- Explore development and testing of new POU/POE devices that may overcome the disadvantages of existing devices.
- Examine readily available household inactivation methods for biological agents (including spore-forming agents), such as microwaving.
- Determine the costs and benefits of further research to identify additional surrogates, considering which agents under which conditions or applications should be prioritized for surrogate development research.

Lessons Learned from Natural Disasters

• Use the remaining data from the experience of Hurricane Katrina to analyze the optimal response and recovery techniques (e.g., water supply alternatives, contingency planning, and infrastructure interdependencies) that would also apply to water security events.

• Integrate experience with decontamination of the distribution system in New Orleans after Hurricane Katrina to improve EPA guidance for water security decontamination.

• Evaluate risk communication strategies related to Hurricane Katrina or other past disaster events to determine if communication strategies related to drinking water safety reached the most vulnerable populations.

• Develop a post-event strategy for learning from future natural disasters affecting water systems. This strategy should support on-site assessments of impacts and interdependencies and evaluations of successes and failures during response and recovery.

Long-Term Priorities

Tools and Data for Emergency Planning and Response

• Continue to develop and maintain the WCIT/CAT databases according to the objectives set forth in the strategic database management plan. Incorporate a mechanism to provide on-going peer review of the data to meet its data quality objectives.

• Continue experimental and computational research to fill critical data gaps in WCIT/CAT, including research on the health effects of both acute and chronic exposure to priority contaminants.

Contingencies for Water Emergencies

• Develop new, innovative technologies for supplying drinking water to affected customers over both short- and long-term water system failures.

Risk Communication and Behavioral Sciences

• Develop a program of interdisciplinary empirical research in behavioral sciences to better understand how to prepare stakeholders for water security incidents. The EPA should support original research that will help address critical knowledge gaps. For example:

  o What are the public's beliefs, opinions, and knowledge about water security risks?

  o How do risk perception and other psychological factors affect responses to water-related events?

  o How can these risks be communicated more effectively to the public?

• Develop a national training program on water-related risk communication planning and implementation for water managers.

Decontamination

• Continue laboratory research to fill the data gaps related to behavior of contaminants in water supply and wastewater systems and methods for decontaminating water infrastructure.

• Continue surrogate research based on the research prioritization determined in collaboration with an interagency working group. The EPA should also explore ways that this surrogate research could assist in responding to everyday agents or to other routes of exposure (e.g., inhalation, inactivating agents on surfaces).

Implementation of Priorities

The EPA has historically been a lead federal agency in understanding the fate and transport of contaminants in the environment and has a clear understanding of the practical concerns of the water sector. Thus, the EPA remains the appropriate lead agency to develop the tools for emergency response and to prioritize the research needed to fill the remaining gaps, with input from key stakeholders. The EPA is also well suited to develop a national training program on water-related risk communication and to evaluate lessons learned from Hurricane Katrina and other past disaster events. However, innovative technology development research, such as the development of novel technologies for supplying water during system failures, should be conducted by other agencies, university researchers, or firms with the greatest expertise. The EPA, instead, should focus its efforts on harvesting information on existing technologies, synthesizing this information for end users, and providing guidance to developers on unique technology needs for water security. Behavioral science research and evaluation research is more appropriately conducted by universities or other federal agencies (e.g., CDC) that have the necessary expertise to complete these tasks. However, the EPA still needs in-house behavioral science experts able to supervise and use this work to best advantage.

CONCLUSIONS AND RECOMMENDATIONS

In this chapter, recommendations are provided for future research directions in the area of water security. Two key water security research gaps—behavioral science and innovative future system design—that were not considered in the short-term planning horizon of the Action Plan are identified. In accordance with the committee's charge (see Chapter 1), short- and long-term water security research priorities are presented in three areas: (1) developing products to support more resilient design and operation of facilities and systems, (2) improving the ability of operators and responders to detect and assess incidents, and (3) improving response and recovery.

The EPA should develop a program of interdisciplinary empirical research in behavioral science to better understand how to prepare stakeholders for water security incidents. The risks of terrorism are dynamic and uncertain and involve complex behavioral phenomena. The EPA should take advantage of existing behavioral science research that could be applied to water security issues to improve response and recovery efforts. At the same time, when gaps exist, the EPA should support rigorous empirical research that will help address, for example, what the public's beliefs, opinions, and knowledge about water security risks are; how risk perception and other psychological factors affect responses to water-related events; and how to communicate these risks effectively to the public.

The EPA should take a leadership role in providing guidance for the planning, design, and implementation of new, more sustainable and resilient water and wastewater facilities for the 21st century. Given the investments necessary to upgrade and sustain the country's water and wastewater systems, research on innovative approaches to make the infrastructure more sustainable and resilient both to routine and malicious incidents would provide substantial dual-use benefits. The EPA should help develop and test new concepts, technologies, and management structures for water and wastewater utilities to meet objectives of public health, sustainability, cost-effectiveness, and homeland security. Specific research topics related to drinking water and wastewater, such as decentralized systems and in-pipe interventions to reduce exposure from contaminants, are suggested.

Recommended research topics in the area of supporting more resilient design and operation of drinking water and wastewater systems include improved processes for threat and consequence assessments and innovative designs for water and wastewater. A thorough and balanced threat assessment encompassing physical, cyber, and contaminant threats is lacking. To date, the EPA has focused its threat assessments on contaminant threats, but physical and cyber threats deserve more attention and analysis because this information could influence the EPA's future research priorities and utilities' preparedness and response planning.

Research suggestions that improve the ability of operators and responders to detect and assess incidents build upon the EPA's current research in the areas of analytical methodologies and monitoring and distribution system modeling. In the short term, the EPA should continue research to develop and refine a first-stage RTMS based on routine water quality parameters with dual-use applications. Long-term research recommendations include the development of innovative detection technologies and cheaper, more accurate RTMSs. To support the simulation models in development, a substantial amount of fundamental research is needed to improve understanding of the fate and transport of contaminants in distribution systems. Based on the number of emerging technologies and agents of interest, the EPA should develop a prioritization strategy for technology testing to optimize the resources devoted to this effort.

Recommendations for future research priorities to improve response and recovery emphasize the sustainability of tools for emergency planning and response (e.g., WCIT/CAT) and improving research on water security contingencies, behavioral sciences, and risk communication. The EPA should also evaluate the relative importance of future laboratory work on surrogate development and address data gaps in the knowledge of decontamination processes and behavior. So far, the EPA has not taken advantage of the many opportunities from Hurricane Katrina to harvest lessons learned related to response and recovery, and the window of opportunity is rapidly closing.

Some of the research recommendations provided in this chapter lie outside of the EPA's traditional areas of expertise. The EPA will need to consider how best to balance intramural and extramural research funding to carry out this research, while maintaining appropriate oversight and input into the research activities. Increasing staff expertise in some key areas, such as physical security and behavioral sciences, will be necessary to build a strong and well-rounded water security research program.

References

Altman, S., B. Bassler, J. Beckwith, M. Belfort, H. Berg, B. Bloom, J. Brenchley, A. Campbell, R. Collier, N. Connell, N. Cozzarelli, N. Craig, S. Darst, R. Ebright, S. Elledge, S. Falkow, J. Galan, M. Gottesman, R. Gourse, N. Grindley, C. Gross, A. Grossman, A. Hochschild, M. Howe, J. Hurwitz, R. Isberg, S. Kaplan, A. Kornberg, S. Kustu, R. Landick, A. Landy, S. Levy, R. Losick, S. Long, S. Maloy, J. Mekalanos, F. Neidhardt, N. Pace, M. Ptashne, J. Roberts, J. Roth, L. Rothman-Denes, A. Salyers, M. Schaechter, L. Shapiro, T. Silhavy, M. Simon, G. Walker, C. Yanofsky, and N. Zinder. 2005. An open letter to Elias Zerhouni. Science 307:1409-1410.

Alupoaei, C.E., J.A. Olivares, and L.H. Garcia-Rubio. 2004. Quantitative spectroscopy analysis of prokaryotic cells: Vegetative cells and spores. Biosensors and Bioelectronics 19:893-903.

ASCE (American Society of Civil Engineers), AWWA (American Waterworks Association), and WEF (Water Environment Federation). 2004a. Interim Voluntary Security Guidance for Water Utilities. Available online at *http://www.awwa.org/science/wise/*. Accessed May 10, 2006.

ASCE, AWWA, and WEF. 2004b. Interim Voluntary Security Guidance for Wastewater/Stormwater Utilities. Available online at *http://www.wef.org/NR/rdonlyres/3BBFF04F-76D0-40BC-9B90-03 DEF844F6CB/0/WEF_Security_Guidance_Final.pdf.* Accessed May 10, 2006.

Ashford, D.A., R.M. Kaiser, M.E. Bales, K. Shutt, A. Patrawalla, A. McShan, J.W. Tappero, B.A. Perkins, and A.L. Dannenberg. 2003. Planning against biological terrorism: Lessons from outbreak investigations. Emerging Infectious Diseases 9:515-519.

ASME (American Society of Mechanical Engineers). 2004. Introduction to Risk Analysis and Management for Critical Asset Protection (RAMCAP). Washington, D.C.: ASME Innovative Technologies Institute, LLC, U.S. Department of Homeland Security.

Berger, M., R. Shiau, and J.M. Weintraub. 2006. Review of syndromic surveillance: Implications for waterborne disease detection. Journal of Epidemiology and Community Health 60:543-550.

Bostrom, A., and R. Lofstedt. 2003. Communicating risk: Wireless and hardwired. Risk Analysis 23:241-248.

Buehler, J.W., R.L. Berkelman, D.M. Hartley, and C.J. Peters. 2003. Syndromic surveillance and bioterrorism-related epidemics. Emerging Infectious Diseases 9:1197-1204.

Bush, G.W. 2003. Directive on Critical Infrastructure Identification, Prioritization, and Protection. Homeland Security Presidential Directive/HSPD-7. Weekly Compilation of Presidential Documents 39:1816-1822.

Bush, G.W. 2004. Directive on Defense of United States Agriculture and Food. Homeland Security Presidential Directive/HSPD-9. Weekly Compilation of Presidential Documents 40:183-187.

Butler, M., and W.J. Weber, Jr. 2005a. Accelerated transformation and deactivation of erythromycin in superheated water. I. Temperature effects, transformation rates, and the impacts of dissolved organic matter. Environmental Science and Technology 39:2294-2300.

Butler, M., and W.J. Weber, Jr. 2005b. Accelerated transformation and deactivation of erythromycin in superheated water. II. Transformation reactions and bioassays. Environmental Science and Technology 39:2301-2306.

CDC (Centers for Disease Control and Prevention). 2003a. Recognition of illness associated with exposure to chemical agents: United States, 2003. Morbidity and Mortality Weekly Report 52:938-940.

CDC. 2003b. Second National Report on Human Exposure to Environmental Chemicals. Atlanta, GA: CDC.

CDC. 2006. Surveillance for early detection of disease outbreaks at an outdoor mass gathering: Virginia, 2005. Morbidity and Mortality Weekly Report 55:71-74.

DHS (Department of Homeland Security). 2006a. National Infrastructure Protection Plan. Available online at *http://www.dhs.gov/xlibrary/assets/NIPP_Plan.pdf*. Accessed January 25, 2007.

DHS. 2006b. Charter: National Science Advisory Board for Biosecurity. Available online at *http://www.biosecurityboard.gov/revised%20NSABB%20charter%20signed%20031606.pdf*. Accessed July 12, 2006.

DiGiovanni, C., B. Reynolds, R. Harwell, E. Stonecipher, and F. Burkle. 2003. Community reaction to bioterrorism: Prospective study of simulated outbreak. Emerging Infectious Diseases 9:708-712.

Dunahee, N., and W.J. Weber, Jr. 2003. Boil water orders: Beneficial or hazardous? Journal of the American Waterworks Association 95:40-45.

EPA (Environmental Protection Agency). 1997. 1996 Clean Water Needs Survey Report to Congress. Washington, D.C.: EPA, Report No. EPA/832/R-97/003.

EPA. 1998. Guidelines for Neurotoxicity Risk Assessment. Risk Assessment Forum, Washington, D.C.: EPA, Report No. EPA/630/R-95/001F.

EPA. 2000. Methods for the Determination of Organic and Inorganic Compounds in Drinking Water, Volume 1. Cincinnati, OH: EPA, Report No. EPA/815/R-00/014.

EPA. 2002. Strategic Plan for Homeland Security. Available online at *http://www.epa.gov/epahome/downloads/epa_homeland_security_str ategic_plan.pdf.* Accessed May 9, 2006.

EPA. 2003a. Board of Scientific Counselors: Communicating Research Results. Available online at *http://www.epa.gov/osp/bosc/pdf/comms 04.pdf.* Accessed July 11, 2006.

EPA. 2003b. Response Protocol Toolbox Module 4: Analytical Guide, Interim Final Draft. Available online at *http://www.epa.gov/ safewater/watersecurity/pubs/guide_response_module4.pdf.* Accessed July 3, 2006.

EPA. 2004a. Water Security Research and Technical Support Action Plan. Cincinnati, OH: Office of Research and Development and Office of Water.

EPA. 2004b. Threat Scenarios for Buildings and Water Systems Report. Cincinnati, OH: National Homeland Security Research Center (NHSRC).

EPA. 2004c. Factoids: Drinking Water and Ground Water Statistics for 2003. Available online at *http://www.epa.gov/safewater/data/pdfs/ data_factoids_2003.pdf.* Accessed May 10, 2006.

EPA. 2004d. Response Protocol Toolbox Module 6: Remediation and Recovery Guide, Interim Final Draft. Available online at *http://www. epa.gov/safewater/watersecurity/pubs/ guide_response_module6.pdf.* Accessed July 3, 2006.

EPA. 2004e. Investing in Our People II, EPA's Strategy for Human Capital, 2004 and Beyond. Available online at *http://www.epa.gov/ oarm/strategy.pdf.* Accessed January 30, 2007.

EPA. 2005a. The Water Security Research and Technical Support Action Plan: Progress Report for 2005. Available online at *http://www. epa.gov/NHSRC/pubs/reportWIPDprogress092905.pdf.* Accessed July 11, 2006.

EPA. 2005b. Fact Sheet: Threat Ensemble Vulnerability Assessment (TEVA) Computational Framework. Available online at *http://www. epa.gov/NHSRC/pubs/fsTEVA111505.pdf.* Accessed May 10, 2006.

EPA. 2005c. Fact Sheet: Chlorine Inactivation of Bacterial Bioterrorism Agents. Available online at *http://www.epa.gov/nhsrc/pubs/ fsChlorine083005.pdf.* Accessed May 10, 2006.

EPA. 2005d. Standardized Analytical Methods for Use During Homeland Security Events, Revision 2.0. Available online at *http://www. epa.gov/nhsrc/pubs/reportSAM092905.pdf.* Accessed May 10, 2006.

EPA. 2005e. Technologies and Techniques for Early Warning Systems to Monitor and Evaluate Drinking Water Quality: A State-of-the-Art Review. Available online at *http://www.epa.gov/nhsrc/pubs/reportEWS120105.pdf.* Accessed May 10, 2006.

EPA. 2005f. ORD Management Multi-Year Plan. Internal document. ORD Management Council, Office of Research and Development.

EPA. 2005g. WaterSentinel System Architecture Draft, Version 1.0 December 12, 2005. Available online at *http://www.epa.gov/ safewater/watersecurity/pubs/watersentinel_system_architecture.pdf.* Accessed July 11, 2006.

EPA. 2005h. Overview of Event Detection Systems for WaterSentinel. Draft, Version 1.0, December 12, 2005. Available online at *http://www.epa.gov/safewater/watersecurity/pubs/watersentinel_eve nt_detection.pdf.* Accessed July 11, 2006.

EPA. 2005i. WaterSentinel Online Water Quality Monitoring as an Indicator of Drinking Water Contamination. Draft, Version 1.0, December 12, 2005. Available online at *http://www.epa.gov/safewater/watersecurity/pubs/watersentinel_wq_monitoring.pdf.* Accessed July 11, 2006.

EPA. 2005j. Wastewater Baseline Threat Document. Cincinnati, OH: NHSRC.

EPA. 2005k. Summary Report: Workshop on National Water Security Communication Symposium, San Francisco, CA, May 20-21, 2004. Available online at *http://www.epa.gov/nhsrc/pubs/reportWS symposium113005.pdf.* Accessed May 10, 2006.

EPA. 2005l. Notice of availability of the document entitled Guidelines for Carcinogen Risk Assessment. Federal Register 70:17765-17817.

EPA. 2006a. Investigation of the Capability of Point-of-Use/Point-of-Entry Treatment Devices as a Means of Providing Water Security. Available online at *http://www.epa.gov/nhsrc/pubs/reportPOU-POE022406.pdf.* Accessed May 10, 2006.

EPA. 2006b. Technical Brief: EPANET Extended to Include Multi-Species Modeling. Available online at *http://www.epa.gov/nhsrc/pubs/tbEPANet051106.pdf.* Accessed July 3, 2006.

EPA. 2006c. Water Sector Security Workshops. Available online at *http://www.epa.gov/nhsrc/pubs/reportWSS061306.pdf.* Accessed July 20, 2006.

EPA. 2006d. Use of Surrogates for *Bacillus anthracis* in the Study of Chlorine Inactivation of Bacterial Agents. Cincinnati, OH: EPA.

Esteban, J., A. Starr, R. Willetts, P. Hannah, and P. Bryanston-Cross. 2005. A review of data fusion models and architectures: Towards engineering guidelines. Neural Computing and Applications 14:273-281.

Fenselau, C., and P.A. Demirev. 2001. Characterization of intact micro-organisms by MALDI mass spectrometry. Mass Spectrometry Reviews 20:157-171.

Fischoff, B. 2005. The psychological perception of risk. In D. Kamien (ed.). The McGraw-Hill Homeland Security Handbook. New York: McGraw-Hill.

Gray, G.M., and D.P. Ropeik. 2002. Dealing with the dangers of fear: The role of risk communication. Health Affairs 21:106-116.

Introne, J.E., I. Levit, S. Harrison, and S. Das. 2005. A Data Fusion Approach to Biosurveillance. 7th International Conference on Information Fusion (FUSION), sponsored by IEEE, pp.1359-1366.

Iqbal, S.S., M.W. Mayo, J.G. Bruno, B.V. Bronk, C.A. Batt, and J.P. Chambers. 2000. A review of molecular recognition technologies for detection of biological threat agents. Biosensors and Bioelectronics 15:549-578.

Ivnitski, D., D.J. O'Neil, A. Gattuso, R. Schlicht, M. Calidonna, and R. Fisher. 2003. Nucleic acid approaches for detection and identification of biological warfare and infectious disease agents. BioTechniques 35:862-869.

Keller, E.F. 2002. Making Sense of Life: Explaining Biological Development with Models, Metaphors and Machines. Cambridge: Harvard University Press.

Lay, J.O., Jr. 2001. MALDI-TOF mass spectrometry of bacteria. Mass Spectrometry Reviews 20:172-194.

Lim, D.V., J.M. Simpson, E.A. Kearns, and M.F. Kramer. 2005. Monitoring for agents of bioterrorism/biowarfare. Clinical Microbiology Reviews 18:583-607.

Lombardo, J.S., H. Burkom, and J. Pavlin. 2004. ESSENCE II and the framework for evaluating syndromic surveillance systems. Morbidity and Mortality Weekly Report 53:159-165.

Mailback, E., and R.L. Parrott (eds.). 1995. Designing Health Messages: Approaches from Communication Theory and Public Health Practice. Thousand Oaks, CA: Sage Publications.

McKone, T.E., and A.W. Deshpande. 2005. Can fuzzy logic bring complex environmental problems into focus? Environmental Science and Technology 39:42A-47A.

Means, E.G. 2002. Drinking water in the new millennium: The risk of underestimating public   perception. Journal of the American Water Works Association 94:28-34.

Meinhardt, P.L. 2005. Water and bioterrorism: Preparing for the potential threat to U.S. water   supplies and public health. Annual Review of Public Health 26:213-237.

Monk, D.J., and D.R. Walt. 2004. Optical fiber-based biosensors. Analytical and Bioanalytical Chemistry 379:931-945.

Morales-Morales, H.A., G. Vidal, J. Olszewski, C.M. Rock, D. Dasgupta, K.H. Oshima, and G.B. Smith. 2003. Optimization of a reusable hollow-fiber ultrafilter for simultaneous concentration of enteric bacteria, protozoa, and viruses from water. Applied Environmental Microbiology 69:4098-4102.

NACWA (National Association of Clean Water Agencies). 2005. Protecting Wastewater Infrastructure Assets: Planning for Decontamination Wastewater: A Guide for Utilities.   Available online at *http://www.epa.gov/nhsrc/pubs/reportDeconGuide 112805.pdf*. Accessed May 10, 2006.

National Cancer Institute. 2002. Making Health Communication Programs Work: A Planner's Guide (also known as the Pink Book). Available online at *http://www.cancer.gov/pinkbook*. Accessed January 30, 2007.

Nesmith, J., and M.J. McKenna. 2005. Who's in charge if bird flu strikes—docs or cops? Atlanta Journal Constitution. Available online at *http://www.ajc.com/today/content/epaper/editions/today/news_34c09175043fd0ef10d0.html*. Accessed July 11, 2006.

Nicholson, W.L., and B. Galeano. 2003. UV resistance of *Bacillus anthracis* spores revisited: Validation of *Bacillus subtilis* spores as UV surrogates for spores of *B. anthracis* Sterne. Applied and Environmental Microbiology 69:1327-1330.

Nicholson, W.L., N. Munakata, G. Horneck, H.J. Melosh, and P. Setlow. 2000. Resistance of *Bacillus* endospores to extreme terrestrial and extraterrestrial environments. Microbiology and Molecular Biology Reviews 64:548-572.

Norton, J.W., and W.J. Weber, Jr. 2005. Breakeven costs of distributed advanced technology water treatment systems. Proceedings of the 2005 American Institute of Chemical Engineers National Conference, October 2005. Cincinnati, Ohio.

NRC (National Research Council). 2002. Making the Nation Safer: The Role of Science and Technology in Countering Terrorism. Washington, D.C.: National Academies Press.

NRC. 2004. A Review of the EPA Water Security Research and Technical Support Action Plan. Washington, D.C.: National Academies Press.

NRC. 2005. Opportunities for Water Security Research: The Aftermath of Hurricane Katrina—Letter Report. Washington, D.C.: National Academies Press.

Office of Homeland Security. 2002. National Strategy for Homeland Security. Available online at *http://www.dhs.gov/interweb/ assetlibrary/nat_strat_hls.pdf.* Accessed May 10, 2006.

Okun, D.A. 1997. Distributing reclaimed water through dual systems. Journal of the American Water Works Association. 89:52-56.

Okun, D.A. 2005. Letter to the editor: Designing future water distribution systems. Journal of the American Water Works Association (6):99-101.

Peruski, A.H., and L.F. Peruski, Jr. 2003. Immunological methods for detection and identification of infectious disease and biological warfare agents. Clinical and Diagnostic Laboratory Immunology 10:506-513.

Rice, E.W., L.J. Rose, C.H. Johnson, L.A. Boczek, M.J. Arduino, and D.J. Reasoner. 2004. Boiling and *Bacillus* spores [letter]. Emerging Infectious Diseases. Available online at *http://www.cdc.gov/ncidod/ EID/vol10no10/pdfs/04-0158.pdf.* Accessed May 9, 2006.

Rice, E.W., N.J. Adcock, M. Sivaganesan, and L.J. Rose. 2005. Inactivation of spores of *Bacillus anthracis* Sterne, *Bacillus cereus*, and *Bacillus thuringiensis* subsp. *israelensis* by chlorination. Applied and Environmental Microbiology 71:5587-5589.

Roberson, J.A., and K.M. Morley. 2005a. Contamination Warning Systems for Water: An Approach for Providing Actionable Information to Decision-Makers. Denver, CO: AWWA.

Roberson, J.A. and K.M. Morley. 2005b. We need to get strategic on water security. Journal of the American Water Works Association 97:42-43.

Rogers, K.R., and A. Mulchandani (ed.). 1998. Affinity Biosensors: Techniques and Protocols. Totowa, NJ: Humana Press.

Rose, L.J., E.W. Rice, B. Jensen, R. Murga, A. Peterson, R.M. Donlan, and M.J. Arduino. 2005. Chlorine inactivation of bacterial bioterrorism agents. Applied and Environmental Microbiology 71:566-568.

Rossi, P.H., M.W. Lipsey, and H.E. Freeman. 2004. Evaluation: A Systematic Approach. Thousand Oaks, CA: Sage Publications.

Sandia National Laboratories. 2001. Risk Assessment Methodology for Security of Dams (RAM-D^{SM}) Field Manual and Training Guide. Albuquerque, NM: Interagency Forum for the Infrastructure Protection (IFIP), Sandia National Laboratories.

Sandia National Laboratories. 2002. Risk Assessment Methodology for Security of High Voltage Power Transmission (RAM-T^{SM}) Field Manual and Training Guide. Albuquerque, NM: Bonneville Power Administration and the Interagency Forum for the Infrastructure Protection (IFIP), Sandia National Laboratories.

Serre, M.L., and G. Christakos. 1999. Modern geostatistics: Computational BME in the light of uncertain physical knowledge—The Equus beds study. Stochastic Environmental Research and Risk Assessment 13:1-26.

Snyder, J.K., A.K. Deb, F.M. Grablutz, S.B. McCammon, W.M. Grayman, R.M. Clark, D.A. Okun, and D. Savic. 2002. Impacts of Fire Flow on Distribution System Water Quality, Design, and Operation. Denver, CO: AWWA and AwwaRF.

Stoto, M.A., M. Schonlau, and L.T. Mariano. 2004. Syndromic surveillance: Is it worth the effort? Chance 17:19-24.

Straub, T.M., and D.P. Chandler. 2003. Towards a unified system for detecting waterborne pathogens. Journal of Microbiological Methods 53:185-197.

Weber, W.J., Jr. 2002. Distributed optimal technology networks: A concept and strategy for potable water sustainability. Water Science and Technology 46:241-246.

Weber, W.J., Jr. 2004. Optimal uses of advanced technologies for water and wastewater treatment in urban environments. Water Science and Technology: Water Supply 4:7-12.

Witte, K., G. Meyer, and D. Martell. 2001. Effective Health Risk Messages: A Step-by-Step Guide. Newbury Park, CA: Sage Publications.

Yu, H., and J.G. Bruno. 1996. Immunomagneticelectrochemiluminescent detection of *Escherichia coli* O157 and *Salmonella typhi-*

murium in foods and environmental water samples. Applied and Environmental Microbiology 62:587-592.

Zhu, L., S. Ang, and W.T. Liu. 2004. Quantum dots as a novel immunofluorescent detection system for *Cryptosporidium parvum* and *Giardia lamblia*. Applied and Environmental Microbiology 70:597-598.

Acronyms

ANL	Argonne National Laboratory
ASCE	American Society of Civil Engineers
AWWA	American Water Works Association
AwwaRF	American Water Works Association Research Foundation
CAT	Consequence Assessment Tool
CDC	Centers for Disease Control and Prevention
CERCLA	Comprehensive Environmental Response, Compensation, and Liability Act
CI^3	Critical Infrastructures Interdependencies Integrator
CPHP	Centers for Public Health Preparedness
DHS	Department of Homeland Security
DOD	Department of Defense
DOT-Net	distributed optimal technology network
EEM	excitation emission matrix
EPA	Environmental Protection Agency
ERDC	Engineering Research and Development Center
ESSENCE	Electronic Surveillance System for the Early Notification of Community-based Epidemics
ETV	Environmental Technology Verification
EWS	early warning system
GC	gas chromatography
GIS	geographic information system
HPLC	high-performance liquid chromatography
HSIN	Homeland Security Information Network
HSPD	Homeland Security Presidential Directive
IPA	Intergovernmental Personnel Act
IRIS	Integrated Risk Information System
ISFET	ion-sensitive field-effect transistor
LD	lethal dose
MS-EPANET	multi species EPANET
NACWA	National Association of Clean Water Agencies
NEMI-CBR	National Environmental Methods Index for Chemical, Biological, and Radioactive Agents
NHSRC	National Homeland Security Research Center

NIH	National Institutes of Health
NRC	National Research Council
ORD	Office of Research and Development
PCR	polymerase chain reaction
PDD	Presidential Decision Directive
POE	point of entry
POU	point of use
QA	quality assurance
QC	quality control
QCM	quartz crystal microbalance
QSAR	Quantitative Structure Activity Relationship
RAM-W	Risk Assessment Methodology for Water Utilities
RODS	Real-time Outbreak and Disease Surveillance
RSS	Rich Site Summary
RTMS	real-time monitoring system
SAB	Science Advisory Board
SCADA	supervisory control and data acquisition
SITE	Superfund Innovative Technology Evaluation
START	Study of Terrorism and Responses to Terror
TEVA	Threat Ensemble Vulnerability Assessment
TTEP	Technology Testing and Evaluation Program
USACE	U.S. Army Corps of Engineers
UV	ultraviolet
VSAT	Vulnerability Self Assessment Tool
WaterISAC	Water Information Sharing and Analysis Center
WaterSC	Water Security Channel
WCIT	Water Contaminant Information Tool
WEF	Water Environment Federation
WERF	Water Environment Research Foundation
WLA	Water Laboratory Alliance
WSCC	Water Sector Coordinating Council
WSTB	Water Science and Technology Board

Appendixes

Appendix A

Letter Report Dated November 10, 2005, to Kim Fox, Director, Water Infrastructure Protection Division, Environmental Protection Agency[1]

---

[1] Attachments A and B of the November 10, 2005 letter were not included in Appendix A because the committee membership is available in the frontmatter of this report and the statement of task can be found in the Summary.

THE NATIONAL ACADEMIES
Advisers to the Nation on Science, Engineering, and Medicine

Water Science and Technology Board
500 Fifth Street, NW
Washington, DC 20001
Phone: 202 334 3422
Fax: 202 334 1961
www.nationalacademies.org/wstb

November 10, 2005

Mr. Kim Fox
Director
Water Infrastructure Protection Division
National Homeland Security Research Center
U.S. Environmental Protection Agency
26 West Martin Luther King Drive
Cincinnati, Ohio 45268

Dear Mr. Fox:

The National Research Council (NRC) would like to offer this letter report on opportunities for water security research afforded by the occurrence of Hurricane Katrina. The NRC's Committee on Water System Security Research (see Attachment A) was created to advise Environmental Protection Agency's (EPA) National Homeland Security Research Center (NHSRC) and its Water Infrastructure Protection Division. This committee builds upon the work of a previous NRC panel, which reviewed the initial water security activities of the NHSRC and issued two reports in 2004.[2] Our new committee has the opportunity to advise the NHSRC as it transitions from a three-year "temporary" research center to a "permanent" center with a longer-term vision and the potential for more complex research endeavors. The committee is currently working to review the progress of EPA's water security research and to identify short- and long-term research priorities (see Attachment B), and its final report is anticipated to be completed in September 2006. However, the committee was also asked to provide letter reports on issues of particular concern for which more immediate advice could be given.

Between our committee's second and third meetings, the nation witnessed the traumatic and catastrophic occurrence of Hurricane Katrina. This natural disaster affected, and in some cases completely destroyed, critical infrastructure including many large and small water and wastewater conveyance and treatment

---

[2] National Research Council. 2004. *A Review of the EPA Water Security Research and Technical Support Action Plan—Parts I and II.* Washington, DC: National Academies Press.

systems in a huge area along the coast of the Gulf of Mexico. Hurricane Katrina also brought two water security issues into dramatic focus: the effects of a total breakdown in drinking water and wastewater systems and the problems brought about by failures of critical interdependent infrastructures (transportation, power, supply chain, etc.).

Hurricane Katrina's lessons are real and not speculative. At our committee's third meeting in October, we discussed with EPA colleagues how the experience of Katrina could be used to mine important lessons and data and thereby advance the nation's abilities to prevent, mitigate, or respond to future water and wastewater system emergencies, including deliberate attacks. It is difficult to imagine prior to an actual event the cascading and compounding impacts on several co-located infrastructure components. The hurricane disaster is a chance to learn from a worst case scenario where entire systems have been simultaneously destroyed and large populations left without service. This is, thankfully, a highly unusual occurrence; therefore, this opportunity should be used to the fullest extent possible to better understand how intentional acts of a similar nature would impact a community and how a community could most effectively recover from such an event. The lessons learned from Hurricane Katrina also have important "dual use" applications for both terrorism and other natural disasters, such as earthquakes.

Several NHSRC personnel who were deployed to the Gulf Coast region were able to see the results of the destruction first hand, and the NHSRC staff clearly recognized the value of the opportunity offered by the Katrina experience. We strongly encourage EPA's NHSRC to organize a systematic review of researchable questions related to the vulnerabilities of water and wastewater systems and examine lessons learned for response and recovery in the aftermath of Hurricane Katrina. Questions are suggested below in three major areas that could serve to focus such a review:

Vulnerabilities:
- What parts of the water and wastewater systems failed (e.g., pumps, treatment plant, the distribution network, or the total system)? What caused the failures?
- What were the key vulnerabilities in the water and wastewater systems revealed by this event? Are these components of the system just as vulnerable to intentional destruction?
- What were the outstanding interdependency issues revealed by this incident (e.g., power, transportation, supply chain)?

Impacts and Mitigation Strategies:
- What steps could have been taken to prevent or mitigate the damage? For example, could an alternate distribution system design, such as built-in redundancy, have significantly reduced the impacts to the system integrity or the time required for system recovery, and if so, what are the costs of such measures?

- What was the extent of the pollution resulting from the shutdown of wastewater systems? What were the public health implications of this pollution? Were available monitoring tools sufficient to assess the situation quickly and notify the public in a timely manner? What design changes or response efforts would have been necessary to contain or limit this pollution?

Response and Recovery:
- Were alternative potable water supplies available in sufficient time to meet the needs of the impacted populations? What characteristics should be developed in future emergency portable systems to better respond to water security incidents or natural disasters? Were there institutional or regulatory barriers to the deployment of alternative supplies?
- If appropriate response materials (e.g., computer programs, written memos, and guidance manuals) had been available, would such materials have been of value in this emergency as it unfolded?
- How effective were the communication strategies related to drinking water safety in reaching the most vulnerable populations? How did EPA's existing risk communication strategies serve this particular incident?
- What special problems were encountered prior to full restoration of water or wastewater service, such as disinfection of the system? What protocols were used to assess when the system was clean and when the water was safe for drinking, and how effective were these protocols?
- How quickly was water or wastewater service restored? What were the most significant barriers to prompt restoration of service, considering both technical and non-technical issues (e.g., availability of standby power, cash-flow to finance the recovery activities)? How could restoration of service be effected more quickly in the future? Do the results of these experiences agree with the RESTORE models currently being developed by the EPA and the U.S. Army Corps of Engineers?
- What were the outstanding workforce and personnel issues related to water and wastewater systems? Which personnel were in shortest supply and in the most sensitive roles such that back-up or redundancy in their tasks would have been beneficial?

Because there is value in understanding the lessons learned in water and wastewater systems of varying size, we suggest that this Hurricane Katrina review should include a number of smaller community water and wastewater systems, not just the systems in New Orleans.

There is a level of urgency about this reconnaissance work as physical evidence and the memory of eye-witnesses begins to fade. EPA clearly recognizes this urgency by the fact that they have recently sought internal funding to support this general initiative, and the committee commends EPA for moving forward quickly.

The above list of suggested research topics is admittedly long and varied, and the committee trusts that EPA will evaluate these time-sensitive opportunities for learning in the context of the overall information needs for water security, considering their other research needs and the availability of funding. The committee chose not to prioritize among the above topics, recognizing that EPA managers can best determine how these opportunities can complement their ongoing efforts.

The committee believes EPA has the expertise to conduct this type of review. We suggest, however, that EPA seek additional input from other relevant organizations and agencies. For example, the Centers for Disease Control and Prevention could contribute their perspective on the public health impacts from the loss of water and wastewater systems during this incident. Professional organizations, such as the Water Environment Foundation, the American Water Works Association, and the American Society of Civil Engineers, could contribute valuable insight from an industry perspective.

In summary, we believe much could be learned from a thorough evaluation of the water and wastewater system failures resulting from Hurricane Katrina that would have direct applicability to the work of EPA's National Homeland Security Research Center. As tragic as this disaster has been, it now provides a unique, real world laboratory in which to study water system failures and service restoration. However, there is a certain urgency to getting such a systematic review of lessons learned underway.

This letter report reflects the consensus of the NRC committee and has been reviewed in accordance with the procedures of the NRC. We hope our report is useful to you as you move forward, and we appreciate the opportunity to advise you on this important and challenging work.

Sincerely,

David Ozonoff, Chair
Committee on Water System
Security Research

Attachment A: Committee membership
Attachment B: Statement of task

Appendix B

WATER SCIENCE AND TECHNOLOGY BOARD

R. RHODES TRUSSELL, *Chair,* Trussell Technologies, Inc., Pasadena, California

MARY JO BAEDECKER, U.S. Geological Survey, Emeritus, Reston, Virginia

JOAN G. EHRENFELD, Rutgers University, New Brunswick, New Jersey

DARA ENTEKHABI, Massachusetts Institute of Technology, Cambridge, Massachusetts

GERALD E. GALLOWAY, Titan Corporation, Arlington, Virginia

SIMON GONZALEZ, National Autonomous University of Mexico, Mexico D.F.

CHARLES N. HAAS, Drexel University, Philadelphia, Pennsylvania

THEODORE L. HULLAR, Cornell University, Ithaca, New York

KIMBERLY L. JONES, Howard University, Washington, D.C.

KAI N. LEE, Williams College, Williamstown, Massachusetts

JAMES K. MITCHELL, Virginia Polytechnic Institute and State University. Blacksburg

ROBERT PERCIASEPE, National Audubon Society, New York, New York

LEONARD A. SHABMAN, Resources for the Future, Washington, D.C.

HAME M. WATT, Independent Consultant, Washington, D.C.

CLAIRE WELTY, University of Maryland, Baltimore County

JAMES L. WESCOAT, JR., University of Illinois at Urbana-Champaign

GARRET P. WESTERHOFF, Malcolm Pirnie, Inc., Fair Lawn, New Jersey

STAFF

STEPHEN D. PARKER, Director
LAUREN E. ALEXANDER, Senior Program Officer
LAURA J. EHLERS, Senior Program Officer

JEFFREY W. JACOBS, Senior Program Officer
STEPHANIE E. JOHNSON, Senior Program Officer
WILLIAM S. LOGAN, Senior Program Officer
M. JEANNE AQUILINO, Financial and Administrative Associate
ELLEN A. DE GUZMAN, Senior Program Associate
ANITA A. HALL, Senior Program Associate
DOROTHY K. WEIR, Senior Program Associate
MICHAEL J. STOEVER, Program Assistant

Appendix C

Biographical Sketches of Committee Members and Staff

David M. Ozonoff, *Chair,* is a professor in and chair emeritus of the Department of Environmental Health at Boston University's School of Public Health. He is also a professor in the Department of Sociomedical Sciences and Community Medicine at Boston University's School of Medicine. His research centers on health effects on communities exposed to various kinds of toxic chemicals, new approaches to understanding the results of small case-control studies, and the effects of exposure misclassification in environmental epidemiology. He has studied public health effects resulting from exposure to a number of contaminated sites. He is the editor-in-chief of the online journal Environmental Health. He is also a member of the Massachusetts Bioterrorism Preparedness and Response Program, and he served on the NRC Committee on Drinking Water Contaminants and the Panel on Water System Security Research. Dr. Ozonoff received his M.D. from Cornell University and his M.P.H. from the Johns Hopkins School of Hygiene and Public Health.

Francis A. DiGiano is a professor of environmental sciences and engineering at the University of North Carolina. Previously, he was also a member of the faculty at the University of Massachusetts, Amherst. His areas of research include water treatment, wastewater treatment, water distribution systems, wastewater reuse, activated carbon adsorption, membrane separations, biodegradation, water quality, natural environmental systems, and engineered environmental systems. Dr. DiGiano has also developed technology for treatment of water and wastewater with an emphasis on physical and chemical separation processes for organic contaminants. His most recent research includes experimental measurements and mathematical modeling of bacterial regrowth in distribution systems and fundamental studies of submerged membrane technology. He received a B.S. in civil engineering from the University of

Massachusetts, Amherst, an M.S. from Tufts University, and a Ph.D. from the University of Michigan, Ann Arbor.

Charles N. Haas is the L.D. Betz Professor of Environmental Engineering, and Head of the Department of Civil, Architectural and Environmental Engineering at Drexel University. His areas of research involve microbial and chemical risk assessment, chemical fate and transport, hazardous waste processing and disposal practices, industrial wastewater treatment, and water and wastewater disinfection processes. Dr. Haas is currently conducting research on disinfection processes, water microbiology, and microbial risk assessment (including of special agents). He has coauthored 14 books or major works on water and wastewater treatment and/or microbial risk assessment. Dr. Haas is currently a member of the Water Science and Technology Board and a fellow of the American Academy of Microbiology, the Society for Risk Analysis, and the American Association for the Advancement of Science. He has served on the National Research Council (NRC) Committee on Public Water Supply Distribution Systems, the Panel on Water System Security Research, and the Committee on Drinking Water Contaminants. Dr. Haas received a B.S. in biology and an M.S. in environmental engineering from the Illinois Institute of Technology and a Ph.D. in environmental engineering from the University of Illinois.

Anna K. Harding is an associate professor in the Department of Public Health at Oregon State University. Her expertise lies in the area of environmental health and includes water quality, public health interventions associated with chemical contamination, community involvement, and communication. Additionally, her research interests include international environmental health and the health of special populations. Dr. Harding's current projects include developing regional exposure scenarios for tribal communities engaged in subsistence lifestyles and the Technical Outreach Services for Communities program. Recent work has also covered topics such as drinking water quality and solar disinfection, evaluating microbial indicators of environmental conditions in rivers, and water quality monitoring for public health and environmental protection. During the past five years, Dr. Harding also worked as a visiting scientist of the Environmental Policy and Risk Management Group at the Pacific Northwest National Laboratory. She received her B.S. in community health and health education from the University of Oregon, Eugene, and her Ph.D. in public health from Oregon State University.

Dennis D. Juranek recently retired as a senior scientist and epidemiologist at the Centers for Disease Control and Prevention (CDC), where he worked since 1970. He worked on various aspects of waterborne diseases including investigation of numerous outbreaks of *Giardia* and *Cryptosporidium*, analysis of national data on waterborne disease outbreaks reported to CDC, and participation in epidemiologic studies to establish a national estimate of the occurrence of waterborne disease. Dr. Juranek worked for several years on issues related to waterborne bioterrorism, and in 2000 he organized and chaired the first multiagency, multiorganizational working group on infectious agents and biotoxins that might be used to intentionally contaminate drinking water. The focus of the working group was to identify the biological agents of greatest concern to drinking water and to identify and resolve data gaps about these agents that could impede a rapid and effective public health response to a contamination event or a terrorist threat against drinking water. Dr. Juranek served on the NRC's Committee on Small Water Supply Systems. He also serves as a faculty member in the Division of Public Health at Emory University. Dr. Juranek received an M.Sc. in medical parasitology from the London School of Tropical Medicine and a D.V.M. in Veterinary Medicine from Colorado State University.

Nancy K. Kim is director of the New York State Department of Health's Division of Environmental Health Assessment, which is responsible for assessing the potential risk for adverse health effects from exposure to toxic substances in homes and communities. Dr. Kim is also an associate professor in the School of Public Health at the State University of New York, Albany. Her research interests include chemical risk assessment, exposure assessment, toxicological evaluations, structure-activity relationships, and quantitative relationships among toxicological parameters. Prior to her current position, Dr. Kim served as the director of the Bureau of Toxic Substance Assessment for the New York State Department of Health and as a research scientist in the Department's Wadsworth Center for Laboratories and Research where she evaluated the toxicity of chemicals and developed human health guidelines for chemicals in air, food, and water. She previously served on the NRC Committee on Drinking Water Contaminants. Dr. Kim received her B.A. in chemistry from the University of Delaware and her M.S. and Ph.D. in chemistry from Northwestern University.

Bruce M. Larson is a career security and risk management professional with 17 years of leadership experience protecting critical infrastructure in the telecommunications, power, water, and government sectors. He currently serves as the Director of Security Programs for American Water and is responsible for integrating and coordinating physical security, information security, crisis management, business continuity, and personnel surety programs across the global operations of RWE Thames Water. RWE Thames is a wholly owned subsidiary of the RWE Group and is the third largest water services provider in the world. Mr. Larson is a council member of the Water Sector Coordination Council.

Daniel V. Lim is Distinguished University Professor of Microbiology in the Department of Biology and the Center for Biological Defense at the University of South Florida. The primary focus of his research is the characterization of virulence mechanisms in pathogenic bacteria and development of innovative technologies to rapidly detect and identify infectious diseases and bacterial pathogens in food, water, air, and on surfaces. His current research involves the development of fiber optic and array biosensor assays for the rapid detection of pathogenic microorganisms. These innovative assays have been used to successfully detect *Bacillus* spores, *E. coli,* and other microorganisms directly from ground beef, apple juice, powder, and potable water. Dr. Lim is a Fellow of the American Academy of Microbiology and recently received the Christopher Columbus Fellowship Foundation's 2004 Homeland Security Award in the biological, radiological, and nuclear field. He received a B.A. in biology from Rice University and a Ph.D. in microbiology from Texas A&M University.

Rudolph V. Matalucci, P.E., is president of Rudolph Matalucci Consultants, Inc., a firm that specializes in infrastructure and architectural surety. Prior to starting his own firm, Dr. Matalucci spent 22 years at Sandia National Laboratories where he served as project engineer and manager on engineering design projects, risk assessment methodology developments, and numerous security technology application projects. He is a nationally recognized expert in the development and implementation of risk assessment methodologies for facilities and infrastructure systems, and of Architectural Surety® approaches and methodologies. Before joining Sandia National Laboratories, Dr. Matalucci served in the U.S. Air Force for 20 years where he directed research and development programs for civil engineering design, construction, testing, and evaluation of U.S. Air Force facilities; directed the development of high explosive simulations for test and evaluation of nuclear weapons air blast and ground shock effects on weapons protective systems; and directed the engineering design, prototype testing, and construction management of major Department of Defense projects. Dr. Matalucci received a B.S. in civil engineering from the University of New Hampshire, and an M.S. and Ph.D. in civil engineering from Oklahoma State University.

David A. Reckhow is professor of civil and environmental engineering at the University of Massachusetts, Amherst. He also serves as the director of the University of Massachusetts Environmental Institute and interim director of the Massachusetts Water Resources Research Center. His research interests include water and wastewater treatment, physical-chemical processes, water chemistry, and water quality modeling, with special emphasis on disinfection byproducts, the use of ozone for water purification, and new techniques for water quality monitoring. He is a board member of the American Water Works Association Research Foundation, and he previously served on the NRC Panel on Water System Security Research. Dr. Reckhow received his B.S. in civil engineering from Tufts University, his M.S. in civil engineering from Stanford University, and his Ph.D. in environmental engineering from the University of North Carolina.

H. Gerard Schwartz, Jr., is currently a senior professor for the Environmental Engineering Science Program at Washington University in St. Louis, Missouri, and a civil/environmental engineering consultant. He was past president of Sverdrup Civil, Inc. and Sverdrup Environmental, Inc., and chair of Jacobs Civil, Inc. Dr. Schwartz was also past president of the Water Environment Federation and founding chair of the Water Environment Research Foundation. His research interests include water and wastewater treatment, study and design of municipal and industrial wastewater treatment systems with special emphasis on high-strength organic wastewater. He is a member of the National Academy of Engineering. Dr. Schwartz received his B.S. and M.S. degrees from Washington University and his Ph.D. from the California Institute of Technology; he also attended Columbia University's business program.

John P. Sullivan, P.E., is Chief Engineer of the Boston Water & Sewer Commission, a position he has held for 16 years. He has 33 years experience in the design and operation of water distribution and wastewater collection systems. Mr. Sullivan's work includes planning, design, construction inspection, and implementing the requirements of various regulations, including the establishment of monitoring programs. He is a Diplomate in the American Academy of Environmental Engineers in the area of water supply and wastewater and a past president of the Association of Metropolitan Water Agencies. Currently, Mr. Sullivan is chair of the Board of Managers for the Water Information Sharing and Analysis Center (WaterISAC) and a member of the Water Sector Coordinating Council. He holds a B.S. degree in Civil Engineering from the University of Massachusetts, Amherst, and an MBA from Northeastern University.

George Tchobanoglous is professor emeritus in the Department of Civil and Environmental Engineering at the University of California, Davis. His principal research interests include wastewater treatment and reuse, wastewater filtration, ultraviolet light disinfection, aquatic wastewater management systems, wastewater management for small and decentralized wastewater management systems, and solid waste management. Most recently, his research efforts have focused on decentralized wastewater management or the collection, treatment, and reuse of wastewater at or near the point of waste generation. He has authored or co-authored over 300 technical publications including 12 textbooks and 2 reference works. He is a former president of the American Association of Environmental Engineers, and he is a member of the National Academy of Engineering. In 2003, he was awarded the Clarke Prize for excellence in water research. Dr. Tchobanoglous received his B.S. degree in Civil Engineering from the University of the Pacific, his M.S. degree in Sanitary Engineering from the University of California, Berkeley, and his Ph.D. in Civil Engineering from Stanford University.

STAFF

Stephanie E. Johnson is a senior program officer with the Water Science and Technology Board. Since joining the NRC in 2002, she has served as study director for five committees, including the Panel on Water System Security Research. She has also worked on NRC studies on contaminant source remediation, the disposal of coal combustion wastes, Everglades restoration, and desalination. Dr. Johnson received her B.A. from Vanderbilt University in chemistry and geology, and her M.S. and Ph.D. in environmental sciences from the University of Virginia on the subject of pesticide transport and microbial bioavailability in soils.

Laura J. Ehlers is a senior program officer for the Water Science and Technology Board. Since joining the NRC in 1997, she has served as study director for eleven committees, including the Committee on Public Water Supply Distribution Systems: Assessing and Reducing Risks, the Committee on Bioavailability of Contaminants in Soils and Sediment, and the Committee on Assessment of Water Resources Research. She received her B.S. from the California Institute of Technology, majoring in biology and engineering and applied science. She earned both an M.S.E. and a Ph.D. in environmental engineering at the Johns Hopkins University. Her dissertation, entitled RP4 Plasmid Transfer among Strains of *Pseudomonas* in a Biofilm, was awarded the 1998 Parsons Engineering/Association of Environmental Engineering Professors award for best doctoral thesis.

Dorothy K. Weir is a research associate with the Water Science and Technology Board. She has worked on a number of studies including Water Quality Improvement in Southwestern Pennsylvania, Everglades Restoration Progress, and Colorado River Basin Water Management. Ms. Weir received a B.S. in biology from Rhodes College in Memphis, Tennessee, and an M.S. degree in environmental science and policy from Johns Hopkins University. She joined the NRC in 2003.